W9-DJB-939

Getting Started in Options

Getting Started in Options

MICHAEL C. THOMSETT

WILEY

JOHN WILEY & SONS

New York • Chichester • Brisbane • Toronto • Singapore

Copyright © 1989 by John Wiley & Sons, Inc.
All rights reserved. Published simultaneously in Canada.

Reproduction or translation of any part of this work
beyond that permitted by Section 107 or 108 of the
1976 United States Copyright Act without the permission
of the copyright owner is unlawful. Requests for
permission or further information should be addressed to
the Permissions Department, John Wiley & Sons, Inc.

This publication is designed to provide accurate and
authoritative information in regard to the subject
matter covered. It is sold with the understanding that
the publisher is not engaged in rendering legal, accounting,
or other professional service. If legal advice or other
expert assistance is required, the services of a competent
professional person should be sought. *From a Declaration
of Principles jointly adopted by a Committee of the
American Bar Association and a Committee of Publishers.*

ISBN: 0-471-61335-5
ISBN: 0-471-61488-2 (pbk.)
Printed in the United States of America

10 9 8 7 6 5 4 3 2 1

Contents

Introduction:
An Investment with Many Faces

Some forms of investment are well understood
by just about everyone. Real estate, for example,
is widely recognized for its historical appreciation and safety. And participation in the stock
market, through direct ownership and the purchase of mutual fund shares, is the most popular
way for individuals to invest.

Other forms are thought to be more speculative and the usual reaction to them is fear. What
do you think when you hear the word *options*?
Some people equate options with complexity
and risk and reject this alternative as being appropriate only for the speculator. But that is not
necessarily true. You overcome the fear of any
new idea by gaining knowledge about it and
then making an informed judgment.

Options have been traded publicly only since 1973. So we have no long-term performance record to use as a reference. We cannot see how options investors fared in the stock market crash of 1929, nor how they came through the bull market of the 1950s. If your parents have owned stocks over the years, their experiences have probably influenced your attitude about that market. This is not the case with options.

Options serve many purposes. You can buy or sell an option as a purely speculative and high-risk device, as a conservative way to protect the value of your holdings, or for a range of purposes in between. To decide how you can profit from the options market, you need to undergo a four-step process of evaluation.

1. You need to master the terminology of this very specialized and complex market. The language of options is foreign even to seasoned stock market investors.

2. You must understand the profile of risk that each type of options investor takes. Are you a conservative investor or a speculator?

3. You must observe the market to see how prices of options change in relation to stocks. You have choices to make as a buyer or seller of stock options. Only by appreciating the benefits, consequences, and risks of different strategies can you proceed with confidence.

4. To succeed as an options investor, you must set a standard for yourself. When will you buy and sell? What is your purpose in investing? And how will your options strategy fit into your total portfolio?

This process is the same one that you should use when first investigating any market. Even buying shares of stock requires the same steps. Successful investing depends on gaining knowledge, identifying risks, tracking the market, and setting your own standards for risk and safety.

This book is designed as an introduction to the options market. It does not recommend that everyone should become a player of the game or that options are always right for everyone. The following chapters explain the terminology and various strategies that you can employ. But ultimately, you must decide whether options can enhance the profits in your portfolio.

Each chapter includes full explanations of terminology and examples of how those words or phrases affect you as an options investor. The various strategies for conservative and speculative investing are then explained in depth, with case histories, illustrations, and identification of different risk profiles.

In many instances, the discussion identifies cost, sales price, and profit, but excludes any mention of a brokerage commission. In reality, you pay a commission every time you buy or sell. The amount will vary by broker and by the number of options traded. As you evaluate options for your own portfolio, the cost of trading should be factored into your own computations.

For any strategy to work, it must be appropriate and comfortable for you. No one idea can work for everyone, and options are no exception to this rule. No matter how practical or foolproof an idea sounds in theory, it must be both profitable and enjoyable for you. Too many would-be investors make their decisions on the advice of others, without first investigating on their own. They fail to research, compare, and analyze in their own best interests.

You will succeed only by first gathering all of

the facts you need to draw an intelligent conclusion. Mere profit is not worth the effort when it comes at the expense of your peace of mind and satisfaction. Real success in the market is a combination of personal accomplishment and financial gain. This book's purpose is to give you the basic information needed to evaluate options and their possible usefulness to you as a successful and knowledgeable investor.

1

Calls and Puts

When describing the different ways to invest money, people usually make a distinction between debt and equity instruments. An example of equity, or ownership, is a share of stock in a publicly traded company. A bond is an example of a debt instrument. When you purchase a bond, you loan money to the issuer.

When you buy shares of stock, you decide how long to hold and when to sell. Stocks have tangible value in that they represent partial ownership in a corporation. Stockholders are entitled to dividends and will benefit from future profits and appreciation in value of the stock, often over many years. And stocks can be transferred to others or used as collateral to borrow money. These features are widely accepted and understood. But are you willing to invest money in something that has no tangible value and that you know will be worthless in less than one year?

option: the right to buy or sell 100 shares of stock at a fixed price and by a specified date

call: an option acquired by a buyer or granted by a seller to buy 100 shares of stock at a fixed price

put: an option acquired by a buyer or granted by a seller to sell 100 shares of stock at a fixed price

These features of options make them especially difficult for many people to accept. You will discover, though, that there may be sound reasons to invest in them. Even the most conservative investor will discover option strategies that can protect their portfolio from loss.

An *option* is a right and nothing more: When you own an option, you do not own stock, but have only the *right* to buy or sell 100 shares of it. That right is yours for as long as you own the option and as long as the option exists, which is nine months or less. There are two types of options: calls and puts. A *call* is the right to buy 100 shares, and a *put* is the right to sell 100 shares. The money you invest in options buys you these rights.

The value of an option increases if the stock moves in the expected direction. A call buyer hopes that the price of the stock will go up, and a put buyer hopes that the price will go down. If they are right and if the timing of those price movements occurs when they think it will, a profit will result.

Why does an option's value change when the stock price moves? The option sets the stock's value at a fixed level. When you buy a call, you take the position, "I am willing to pay for the right to buy this stock at a fixed price at some point in the future." If that stock's price ends up higher than the identified fixed price, then the call becomes more valuable.

The same argument applies for a put buyer, but in reverse. When you buy a put, your position is, "I am willing to pay for the right to *sell* this stock at a fixed price at some point in the future." If the stock's price ends up lower than that fixed price, the put becomes more valuable.

THE CALL OPTION

A call is the right to buy 100 shares of stock at a fixed price per share and within a limited period of time. As a call buyer, you acquire that right, and as a call seller, you grant the right to someone else.(See Figure 1–1.)

Calls are not unique to the stock market. They are used in many situations, although they are not always referred to as calls.

Example: The owner of a house leases it to a tenant under terms known as a lease with the option to buy. A monthly payment includes two parts: rent and a partial deposit toward a future down payment. The future price of the home is fixed at $95,000, but it must be purchased within three years. If the tenant decides not to buy the house, the accumulated deposit will be returned to him. As long as the option is in effect, the owner cannot raise the agreed upon price.

Three years later, real estate prices have risen dramatically, and the market value of the house is estimated at $110,000, or $15,000 higher than

buyer: an investor who purchases a call or a put option (If the value of the option rises, the buyer will realize a profit by selling the option at a price above the purchase price.)

seller: an investor who sells an option (If the value of the option falls, the buyer will realize a profit by buying, or canceling, the option at a price below the original sales price.)

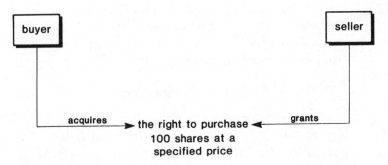

FIGURE 1–1. The Call Option

market value: the value of an investment as of a specified time or date, or the price that buyers are willing to pay and sellers are willing to receive for a stock or option

contract: a single option, including the attributes of that option: identification of the stock on which it is written, the cost of the option, date the option will expire, and the fixed price at which the stock will be bought or sold if the option is exercised

expiration date: the date that an option becomes worthless (Every option contract includes a specified date in the future on which it expires.)

the agreed price. So the owner approaches the tenant with an offer: "I'd like to cancel your option to buy. I will return your accumulated deposit and add an extra $7,000 if you will agree to cancel." The tenant responds, "I am still interested in buying the house for $95,000. If I go somewhere else, I'll have to pay $110,000. So I will allow you to cancel our agreement, but only if you're willing to pay me $12,000."

This type of option can be negotiated between the owner (seller of the option) and the tenant (purchaser of the option). Because the underlying property has increased in value, the option has also become a valuable asset. If the buyer and tenant can agree upon a price, the option will be canceled. Otherwise, the tenant has the right to purchase the house for $95,000.

Listed options—those traded publicly over the New York, Chicago, Pacific, American, and Philadelphia stock exchanges—are not negotiated in the same way. Prices are established strictly by the auction market, under the same principles that govern the buying and selling of stocks. An increase in demand causes prices to rise, and a decrease causes them to fall. So *market value* is the price that buyers are willing to pay and sellers are willing to receive. Under this system, a call buyer or seller will always have a ready market and will be able to cancel an option *contract* at the current market price.

How Call Buying Works

As the owner of a call, you are not obligated to buy the stock. You have until the *expiration date* of the option to decide what action to take. This decision will depend on movement in the stock's market value.

1. If the market value of the underlying *stock* rises, the option's market value will also rise. So you can either buy the stock at the fixed price per share, which is called *exercising the option*, or sell the call for a higher price. In either event, you make a profit. The fixed price of the stock is referred to as the *striking price of the option*.

Example: You buy a call for $100 that entitles you to buy 100 shares of stock at a fixed price of $35 per share. A month later, the option is near expiration. The stock is worth $40 per share, and the option's price is $600. You can exercise the option and buy 100 shares of the stock at $35, which is $5 per share below current value. Or you can sell the call for $600 and take your profit of $500 on the investment.

2. If the market value of the stock does not change, you must decide whether to sell the call before its expiration date (after which the option will be worthless) or to hold onto it (hoping the stock's value will rise before the expiration date). The option is a *wasting asset*. If the market value of the stock does not change during the time you own the call, the option will eventually lose its value. The *premium*—the current market value of the option—near expiration will be lower than it was at the time you purchased it.

Example: You paid $300 for a call several months ago. It will expire this month and is now worth only $100. You can sell and take a loss of $200 or hold until just before expiration (hoping the stock's price will move upward). If you do not take action by the expiration date, the option will become worthless.

underlying stock (also called underlying security): the stock on which the option grants rights to buy or sell (Every stock option refers to a specific, underlying stock.)

exercise: the act of buying or selling stock at the fixed price specified in the option contract (When a buyer exercises an option, he or she purchases stock at a price lower than market value; when a put is exercised, he or she sells stock at a price higher than market value.)

striking price: the price of stock indicated in the option contract (For example, when an option specifies a striking price of $45 per share, regardless of the actual market value of the stock, that option can be exercised at the striking price of $45 per share.)

wasting asset: any asset that will decline in value over time (An option is a wasting asset because it will be worth its intrinsic value on expiration day and worthless after expiration day.)

premium: the current price of an option, which buyers pay and sellers receive at the time of the transaction (The amount is expressed as the amount per share, without dollar signs; for example, when a broker states that an option "is at 3," that means its premium is $300.)

3. If the market value of the stock falls, the call will also decline in value. If the drop in the stock's price is substantial, your call option will be worth much less than the price you paid. You can sell and accept only a small part of your original premium or allow the option to expire worthless.

Example: You bought a call for $200 several months ago. But the stock fell, and your option is now worth only $50. You can sell the option and accept a $150 loss or hold it until immediately before expiration (hoping for a last minute change in the stock's market value). If you wait beyond the option's expiration date, you will lose the entire investment.

Buying a call is risky. Because it has only a limited life, you could lose the entire amount spent for the purchase. But it does allow you to benefit from rising prices without requiring you to invest a large sum of money.

Example: You gain control of 100 shares of stock selling for $80 per share by purchasing a single call. Buying the stock would cost you $8000, but buying a call costs much less. The price depends on the current market value of the stock compared to the features of the call itself. (The pricing of calls will be explained later in this chapter.)

You invest much less money, but stand to gain the same amount if the stock rises. You also reduce the risk of loss, because you can never lose more than the price of the call itself.

Example when the stock price rises: You buy a call for $200, which gives you the right to buy 100 shares of stock at $80 per share. If the stock's market value rises above $80, your call will then rise almost dollar for dollar with the stock. So if the stock goes up $4, to $84 per share, your call rises $4 per option as well, and you can earn a profit of $400. That's the same profit you would have realized by investing $8,000 to buy 100 shares.

Example when the stock price falls: You buy a call for $200, which gives you the right to buy 100 shares of stock at $80 per share. By the expiration date of the option, that stock has fallen to only $68 per share. You lose your $200 investment. However, if you had bought 100 shares, your loss at this point would be $1200 (cost of $80 per share, less current value of $68). Compared to buying the stock directly, your option risks are smaller. Your main disadvantage is the time limit. A stockholder has the right to hold those shares indefinitely and to wait for the price to rise again. As an option buyer, you have only a few months to realize a profit.

If a significant drop in price is temporary, the stockholder can afford to wait. During that time, the stockholder is also entitled to dividends that might be declared by the company. And the stock can be pledged as collateral in a brokerage margin account to buy additional shares.

The real advantage of buying calls is that you are not required to deposit a large sum of money, and yet you control the same number of shares. Your losses are limited, but only during the period of the option's life.

How Call Selling Works

A call seller *grants* or gives away the right to buy 100 shares. As a call seller, you receive a payment for granting that right, but must be willing to actually sell 100 shares at a fixed price. This approach to the options market has much greater risks.

As a buyer, the decision to hold, sell, or exercise the option is yours. But as a seller, someone else will make the decision. Sellers will make or lose money in one of the following ways.

1. If the market value of the stock rises, the call also becomes more valuable. The buyer might exercise the option, which means that he or she will "call" 100 shares of stock at the agreed fixed price. You would have to deliver those shares.

Example: You sell a call for 100 shares at $40 per share. A month later, the market value of that stock is $46 per share. If the buyer exercises the option, you will be obligated to deliver 100 shares at $6 below current market value. If you own those shares, you must give them up at the fixed price of $40 each.

Example: Given the same circumstances, you are obligated to deliver 100 shares but do not own them. You will be required to buy them at today's price ($46 per share) and then give them up at the agreed fixed price ($40 per share)—for a loss of $600.

2. If the market value of the stock remains at approximately the same level, the value of the call declines over time because it is a wasting asset. You can cancel the option by buying it at a lower price than you paid. This action results in a profit for you.

Example: You sell a call and receive payment of $400. Several months later, the stock is at about the same value as the option's fixed price, and the option is worth only $100. You can cancel the option by buying it and realize a profit of $300. Or you can allow it to expire worthless, in which case the entire sales price of $400 is a profit to you.

3. If the market value of the stock falls, the option also declines in value. You can either wait until expiration, when the call will expire worthless (meaning you keep the entire amount you received as a seller), or you can cancel the call by buying it and also make a profit.

Example: You sell a call and receive payment of $500. The stock falls far below the option's fixed price and a recovery seems unlikely. If the stock's market value is still at or below the fixed price of the call at the time of expiration, the entire $500 is profit. Or you can cancel your obligation as a seller by buying the contract at its current price. In that case, the difference between your initial sales price and the current buying price is your profit.

How can you sell something before you buy it? The call seller executes the transaction in a way that, to most people, is backward. You understand a transaction involving a purchase, followed by a sale. But the process can also work in reverse. The same technique can be used for selling stocks directly. For example, an investor, expecting prices to fall, instructs a broker to sell 100 shares of stock he does not own. In this technique, known as short selling, he "borrows" the stock from the broker to sell at an anticipated lower price. If correct, he can later cancel the position by buying the shares at the lower price. But if he's wrong, he can only cancel the

short position: the
status of any in-
vestment that has
been sold and is
currently held,
pending an offset-
ting purchase (to
cancel the position)
or expiration

long position: the
status of any in-
vestment that has
been bought and is
currently held,
pending an offset-
ting sale (to cancel
the position) or ex-
piration

"short sale" by buying the shares at a higher price than at the time of the original sale.

Short sales occur outside of the stock market every day. Some examples are as follows:

- An art dealer sells limited edition prints, but has only one print that she shows customers. After sales are made, she orders and pays for more prints and then delivers them to the purchasers.
- A car dealer fixes the price of a car with special features that has not yet been manufactured.
- A contractor sells hundreds of tract homes by showing a model before the homes for sale have been built.

When you sell an option, you are said to be in a *short position*. In comparison, a buyer assumes a *long position*.

THE PUT OPTION

A put is the opposite of a call. It is the right to sell 100 shares of stock at a fixed price per share and within a limited period of time. As a put buyer, you acquire that right, and as a put seller, you grant the right to someone else. (See Figure 1–2.)

Buying and Selling Puts

Buyers of puts expect the underlying stock to fall in value. If the stock's market value does fall, the put's value will increase, and if the stock rises, the put's value decreases. As a put buyer, you will have three possible outcomes.

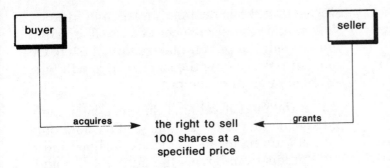

FIGURE 1–2. The Put Option

1. If the market value of the stock rises, the value of the put falls in response. You can either sell the put for a lower price and take a loss or hold onto it (hoping the stock will fall before the expiration date).

Example: You buy a put for $100, expecting the value of the stock to fall. But instead, it rises, and the put's value falls to $25. You can sell and take a loss of $75. Or you can hold until expiration, hoping the stock will rebound. If it does not, the option becomes worthless at expiration.

2. If the market value of the stock stays at approximately the same value as when the put was bought, the value of the put falls over time since it is a wasting asset. The closer to expiration, the less is its value. You can either sell the put and take a partial loss or hold onto it (hoping the stock's market value will fall before expiration of your put).

Example: You buy a put for $300, expecting the stock to fall in market value. But near expiration, the stock price is about the same. However, your put has declined in value to $100. Now realizing your chances of a profit are slim, you can sell the put and take a loss of $200. Or you can wait, hoping the stock's price will fall before expiration of the put.

3. If the market value of the stock falls, the put's value increases. You may either hold onto the put (hoping for further stock declines and more profits from buying the put) or sell it and take a profit. You also have the right to sell 100 shares of stock before expiration at the fixed price, which is higher than current market value.

Example: You buy a put for $50, after which the stock's price falls to $7 below the fixed price specified by the option. That option rises to a value of $750. You have three choices: You can sell the option and realize an immediate profit of $700. You can hold onto the option (hoping for further declines in the stock's price), but risk a loss of profits if the stock rises. Or you can exercise the option and sell 100 shares at the fixed price.

Example: You own 100 shares of stock and buy a put for $50 that fixes the price at $40 per share. A few weeks later, the stock's price falls to $33 per share. The option's value rises to $750. You can sell the option and take a $700 profit, thereby offsetting the loss in the stock you own. Or you can exercise your option and sell the stock for $40 per share, or $7 above current market value. In this case, your $50 investment protected your 100 shares from a price decline and allowed you to sell at a fixed price when that market value fell.

Rather than buying puts in the hope that stock prices will fall, you can also be a put seller. Un-

der this plan, you grant someone else the right
to sell 100 shares of stock to you at a fixed price.
At the time you sell, you receive a premium
equal to the put's current market value. Like the
call seller, you do not have as much control over
the outcome of your investment, since the buyer
will decide whether to exercise the put you sold
him.

Example: You sell a put with a *striking price*
—the fixed price—of $35. You receive $250 at
the time of sale. The stock's market value is now
$36 per share, and you do not expect it to fall
below the striking price. As long as the market
value of the stock remains at or above that striking price, the put will not be exercised, and you
will make a profit. You can cancel the contract
by purchasing it at a lower price than you received or by waiting for it to expire worthless.

If the market value of the underlying stock
does fall below the $35 striking price, the put
option will increase in value nearly dollar for
dollar with the falling stock. But for a seller, this
change in market value is a negative factor.

Example: Just before expiration, the stock is
worth $29 per share. The buyer can exercise the
put you sold and force you to buy 100 shares at
$35 per share ($6 per share above current market
value). If you want to avoid exercise, you can
also cancel the put by buying it for $600, or at a
loss of $350.

Selling options is a higher risk strategy than
buying. Because options lose value as the expiration date approaches, you have an advantage as
a seller: Time is on your side. But if the movement in the underlying stock is opposite what
you expected, you stand to lose money. Sudden

changes in the market value of stock can occur at any time, and the more *volatility* in the market and in the underlying stock, the greater are your risks as a seller.

A call seller's risks are unlimited, since a stock's value can rise indefinitely. The put seller's risk is *finite*—that is, limited to the difference between the contingent price of the stock and zero. A stock cannot fall below a zero value.

THE UNDERLYING STOCK

Option values change in direct relationship to the market value of the underlying stock. Every option is married to the stock of a specified company, and how the investor fares depends on how that stock's value changes in the future.

As shown in Table 1–A, you will consider price movement in the underlying security as a positive or as a negative, depending on whether you are a buyer or a seller and on whether you are involved with calls or puts.

Example: You purchase a call for a premium of 3 points (in the options market, "3" means the option's premium is $300), with a striking price of $40. At that time, the underlying stock is also at $40 per share. This condition is de-

TABLE 1–A Price Movement in the Underlying Security

	Increase in Price	Decrease in Price
Call buyer	positive	negative
Call seller	negative	positive
Put buyer	negative	positive
Put seller	positive	negative

scribed as *at the money*. That is, the stock increases in value to $46, and the option increases in value by $600 ("6" higher than the value at the time you purchased it). Whenever the stock's current market value exceeds the striking price of a call, it is *in the money*. If the price falls below the striking price of the call (a condition known as *out of the money*), the call's value will also fall.

Figure 1–3 shows the in-, at-, and out-of-the-money ranges in comparison to a striking price of a call. For a put, the terms are reversed. When the current market value of the underlying stock is *lower* than the striking price of the put, it is in the money, and when that value is higher than the striking price of the put, it is out of the money.

at the money: a condition in which the market value of the underlying security is identical to the striking price of the option

in the money: a condition in which the market value of the underlying stock is higher than the call's striking price or lower than the put's striking price

out of the money (the opposite of "in the money"): a condition in which the market value of the underlying stock is lower than the call's striking price or higher than the put's striking price

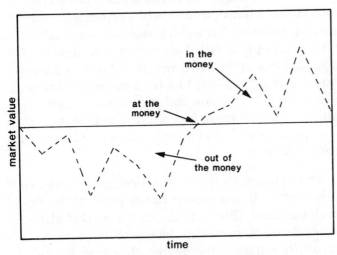

the underlying stock

FIGURE 1–3. Market Value of the Underlying Stock

The approximate dollar-for-dollar movement of an option occurs whenever an option is in the money. But when it is out of the money, changes in the value of the stock will not necessarily have an equal effect on the option premium.

Example: You buy a put with a striking price of $40, paying 2 (total premium, $200). At that time, the stock's price is $44. A few weeks later, the stock's price falls to $41, a decline of 3 points. But your put's value has increased by only 1 ½ points, and its current value is 3 ½. The stock continues to fall, going in the money (below the striking price of $40). The value of your put increases nearly dollar for dollar with the decline of the stock's value—as long as it's in the money.

Example: You buy a call with a striking price of $25, paying 3. The stock's current price is $24. The following week, the stock's price rises to $25, but your option is still available for the same premium. If the stock rises another half point, the option will follow suit. If it goes up 7 points, your option will rise in value by an additional 7 points ($700) to a total current value of $1050, or 10 ½. If you sell the option at that point, you will make a profit before broker's commission of $750 (current value of $1050, less cost of $300).

volatility: a measure of the degree of change in a stock's market price during a twelve-month period, stated as a percentage (To compute, you subtract the lowest price from the highest price during the twelve months and divide the difference by the annual low.)

volume: the level of trading activity in a stock, an option, or in the market as a whole

The value of in the money options is inescapably related to movement in the price of the underlying stock. But "value" in the market also depends upon two other factors. First is *volatility*—that is, the degree of change in the value of both the option and the underlying stock. Second is the time remaining from your transaction date until expiration. Changes in value are often anticipated or accompanied by changes in *volume*, the level of trading activity in a stock or option, or in the market as a whole. (The level of volume in an underlying stock will affect an option's premium.)

TIME VALUE AND INTRINSIC VALUE

A listed option's premium consists of two parts. Its *intrinsic value* is that part represented by the degree that it is in the money. Any difference is *time value*, which declines over the life of the option so that, at the point of expiration, it is zero. The longer the time until that expiration date, the higher is the time value premium.

Example: An option initially goes on the market with a premium of 3 ($300). Its striking price is $45 per share, and the current market value of the underlying stock is also $45. Because it is not in the money, the entire option premium is time value. You can expect this time value to decrease over the coming nine months. The stock's market value ranges from $44 to $47 per share during that time and also at the point of expiration. It is worth $46, or $1 above the strike price. The option's premium at expiration is 1 ($100).

The comparison of option premium and the market value of the underlying stock in Table 1–B reveals the direct relationships between intrinsic value, the market price of the underlying stock, and the declining nature of time value. Figure 1–4 shows how movement in the underlying stock is identical to the option's intrinsic value. When the stock is at the money or out of the money, there is no intrinsic value. And

intrinsic value: the amount the option is in the money (An at-the-money or out-of-the-money option has no intrinsic value.)

time value: the option's premium above any intrinsic value (When an option is at the money or out of the money, the entire premium represents time value.)

listed option: an option traded on a public exchange (Listed options are traded on the New York, Chicago, Pacific, American, and Philadelphia stock exchanges.)

TABLE 1–B The Declining Time Value of an Option

Month	Stock Price	Option Premium (Striking Price of $45)		
		Total Value	Intrinsic Value[1]	Time Value[2]
1	$45	$3	$0	$3
2	47	5	2	3
3	46	4	1	3
4	46	3	1	2
5	47	4	2	2
6	44	2	0	2
7	46	2	1	1
8	45	1	0	1
9	46	1	1	0

[1]Intrinsic value reflects the price difference between the stock's current market value and the option's striking price.

[2]Time value is greatest when the expiration date is farthest away and declines as expiration approaches.

when it is in the money, the intrinsic value matches the degree exactly. You can also see how time value depreciates over the life of the option.

The total amount of premium might vary between two different stocks at the same price due to perceptions of value. For example, two corporations have current options with striking prices of $55, and both are valued at $58 per share. But the option premium is 5 for one stock, and 7 for the other.

Time value for different stocks will not always change in an identical manner. The difference in perception among investors affects the total premium. For example, one company might be ru-

time value and intrinsic value

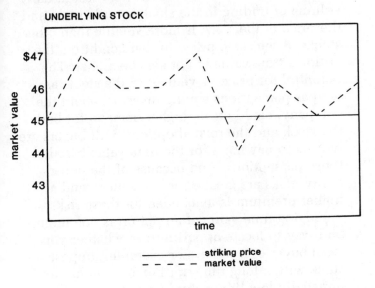

UNDERLYING STOCK

market value

$47
46
45
44
43

time

———— striking price
– – – – – market value

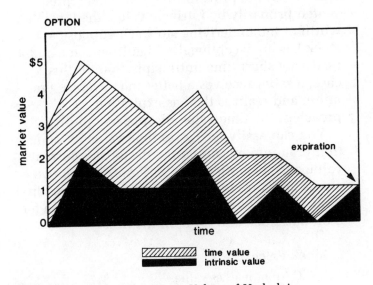

OPTION

market value

$5
4
3
2
1
0

expiration

time

//////// time value
■ intrinsic value

FIGURE 1–4. Time and Intrinsic Values of Underlying
Stock and Options

mored as a takeover candidate. As a result, daily volume of trading in the stock is quite high, and the price of the stock is more volatile than other stocks of the same price. In that condition, the option's time value might also be higher. The *potential* for price movement in the stock, as well as perceptions among investors about the company, could create higher demand for both the stock and the related options. Call buyers are willing to pay more for the time value based on those perceptions. And because of the uncertainty, risks are greater for call sellers, and a higher premium is demanded for those risks.

Judging time value of an option is one important way to locate opportunities, whether you are a buyer or a seller. For example, suppose a stock with a long time until expiration has an unusually low time value. As a buyer, you recognize that the price for that option is represented primarily by intrinsic value, the tangible worth of the underlying stock. Or suppose a stock has an exceptionally high time value and a relatively short time until expiration. In this case, a seller receives a better than average premium and realizes that, as expiration approaches, the time value disappears rapidly.

You can easily recognize time value in an option premium by comparing the stock's current value and the option's price. For example, two stocks are currently priced at $47 per share. Options with striking prices of $45 are available for 3 on one stock and for 5 on the other.

Stock Price:

Current market value	$47
Less striking price	45
Intrinsic value	$2

Option Premium:

Option #1	$3
Less intrinsic value	<u>2</u>
Time value	$1

In the next chapter, striking price, expiration date, and exercise will be explained relative to how they affect your option strategies.

2

Opening, Closing, and Tracking the Option

Every option is described by four attributes that are collectively called the *terms* of the option. These are the striking price, expiration date, type of option (call or put), and the underlying stock.

In evaluating an option for risk and potential profits, the point of view of an option seller is different than that of the buyer. For each of the four terms of an option, what is an advantage to one is a disadvantage to the other.

terms: the complete description of an option, including the underlying security, type (call or put), striking price, and expiration month

1. *Striking price.* If you are a buyer, the striking price tells you at what price you will buy (call) or sell (put) 100 shares of stock in the event you decide to exercise the option. If you are a seller, the striking price tells you at what price you will have to sell 100 shares of stock (if you have sold a call) or buy 100 shares of stock (if you have sold a put) in the event your option is exercised by the buyer.

class: all options traded on a single underlying security, including different striking prices and expiration dates

series: a group of options sharing identical terms

cycle: the series of expiration dates on the options of a particular underlying stock (There are three cycles, according to expiration dates: (1) January, April, July, and October; (2) February, May, August, and November; and (3) March, June, September, and December.)

2. *Expiration date.* Every option exists for a limited number of months. It must be canceled, exercised, or allowed to expire by that expiration date. The limited life of the option increases risks; it also provides opportunities. A buyer, for example, must realize a profit before expiration, or the option investment will lose money. A seller, though, benefits if the option stays out of the money all the way to expiration. In that case, the investment is profitable since the option will not be exercised.

3. *Type of option.* The third term specifies whether the option is a call or a put. You will recall that a call is the right to buy 100 shares, and a put is the right to sell. If you believe the underlying stock will increase in value within the expiration period of an option, you would want to buy calls or sell puts, and if you believe the stock's value will fall, you would want to sell calls or buy puts.

4. *Underlying stock.* Every stock option is identified with a specific company's stock. Considering the large number of stocks available on the various exchanges and over the counter, only a limited number of them have listed options. All options available on one underlying stock are referred to as a single *class* of option. And all of those options with the same terms (striking price, expiration date, call or put, and underlying stock) are considered a single *series*.

A Note on The Expiration Cycle

Expiration for the options of a single underlying stock occurs within one of three expiration *cycles*. Every stock with listed options falls into one of these. The three cycles have expiration dates in:

- January, April, July, and October
- February, May, August, and November
- March, June, September, and December

In addition to these fixed expiration cycle dates, active options might also be available for one- or two-month terms for the immediate future. For example, on issues with options expiring in the cycle month of April, there might also be contracts available on a short-term basis, so that in February, you can buy or sell options with expirations in March, April, July, or October.

The expiration of an option always occurs on the third Saturday of the expiration month. However, an order for cancellation or exercise of an open contract must take place by the Friday before expiration date, no later than 5:30 P.M. (New York time), which is the latest possible expiration time.

Example: You have purchased a January call and want to sell it before the expiration date. The third Saturday is the 17th of January. You must place your sell order on Friday, January 16, which is the *last trading day* for the options in that class. Otherwise, the option will expire and be worthless the following day when the market is closed.

expiration time: the latest possible time to place an order for cancellation or exercise, which is 5:30 P.M. (New York time) on the Friday immediately preceding the third Saturday of the expiration month

last trading day: the Friday preceding third Saturday of the expiration month of an option

OPENING AND CLOSING OPTION TRADES

Every option trade you make must specify all of the four terms: striking price, expiration date, call or put, and underlying stock. If any one of the terms changes, it becomes a different option.

Whenever you make a trade, the terms must

open position: the status when a purchase (long) transaction or a sale (short) transaction has been made (The position remains open until cancellation, expiration, or exercise.)

opening purchase transaction: a transaction executed to buy, also known as "going long"

opening sale transaction: a transaction executed to sell, also known as "going short"

be fully described. Later in this chapter, you will see how actual trades are done by way of a coded abbreviation involving symbols. For now, it is important to understand that there are two ways to open an option's position (buying and selling) and three ways to close an option's position (cancellation, exercise, or expiration).

Whenever you have bought an option and it has not yet closed, you are in an *open position*. If you buy an option to open a position, it is called an *opening purchase transaction*. And if you start out by selling an option, that is called an *opening sale transaction*.

Example: You buy a March call, which is an opening purchase transaction. As long as you still own that call, it remains open. It is closed by sale, exercise, or expiration.

Example: You sell a September call, which is an opening sale transaction. Before the expiration date next September, one of three events can occur: The option will be exercised by the buyer, and you will have to sell 100 shares at the striking price. You will cancel the open position by buying the same option. Or it will expire and be worthless.

The actions or events that change an open position to a *closed position* are called closing transactions. When you are "long" (meaning you previously bought an option) and you sell the option, that is called a *closing sale transaction*. And if you are "short" (meaning you previously sold an option) and you subsequently buy the option, that is called a *closing purchase transaction*.

closed position: the status of an option that has been canceled or exercised or is expired

All options are subject to a one-day settlement. That means that whenever you buy, you must make payment on the business day after the trade. And if you sell, the proceeds are paid to your account on the next business day. In comparison, stock purchases and sales settle in five business days.

Example: Several months ago, you purchased a March call. Today, you phone your broker and instruct her to sell the option. The sale is a closing sale transaction since it cancels your ownership of the option. The proceeds will be credited to your account on the following business day.

Example: You previously sold a September put. During the life of the option, the buyer can exercise and force you to buy 100 shares at the striking price. Or you can execute a closing purchase transaction, which will cancel your short position. In that case, you will be required to pay for the closing purchase on the next business day. If neither exercise nor cancellation occur, the option will become worthless next September.

closing sale transaction: a sale to close a previous long position (For example, if you previously bought an option, a closing sale transaction cancels that position.)

closing purchase transaction: a purchase to close a previous short position (For example, if you previously sold an option, a closing purchase transaction cancels that position.)

DEFINING POSSIBLE OUTCOMES OF CLOSING OPTIONS

Every option will be canceled by an offsetting transaction, an exercise, or an expiration. The results of each are different for buyers and sellers.

Results for the Buyer

1. If you cancel your open position with a closing sale transaction, you receive payment. If the price is higher than your original purchase, you realize a profit; if lower, it's a loss.

2. If you exercise the option, you receive or sell 100 shares of the underlying stock at the striking price.
3. If you allow the option to expire, you lose the entire premium invested in the option.

Results for the Seller

1. If you cancel your open position with a closing purchase transaction, you must pay the premium on the following business day. If the price is lower than your original sale, you realize a profit; if higher, it's a loss. This outcome is opposite that for a buyer.
2. If the option is exercised, you must deliver 100 shares of the underlying stock at the striking price (if a call) or accept 100 shares at the striking price (if a put).
3. If the option expires worthless, you earn a profit. Your open position is canceled by

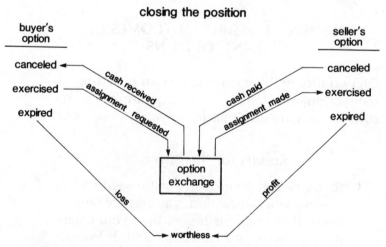

FIGURE 2–1. Outcomes of Closing the Position

the expiration, and the entire premium you received upon sale is yours to keep.

These outcomes are summarized in Figure 2–1. Notice that buyers and sellers have opposite results to a closed option. The buyer receives cash upon sale, while the seller pays. The buyer chooses to exercise the option, while the seller is on the passive side of that decision. And upon expiration, the buyer loses money, while the seller profits.

EXERCISING AN OPTION

Options transactions occur through the exchange on which the option is listed. While several different exchanges handle trading of options, the Options Clearing Corporation (OCC) ensures the orderly settlement of all listed option contracts. When a seller notifies the OCC of the desire to exercise (through a broker and then through the listing exchange), the order is assigned to a buyer by the OCC. Notification is sent to a *clearing member*—a brokerage firm that handles its customers' accounts.

In this way, sellers do not have to rely directly on buyers to honor their obligations under the option contract. The OCC depends on clearing members to enforce *assignment*. Since there is no specific matching of open positions between buyers and sellers as long as options remain unexercised, the seller whose option is actually exercised is selected on either a random basis or on the basis of first-in, first-out (the earliest buyer will be the first one exercised). Upon exercise of the option, 100 shares must be delivered. *Delivery* is the physical movement of stock from one owner to another.

assignment: the act of exercise against a seller (When the buyer exercises an option, it is assigned to a seller, usually on a random basis.)

delivery: physical movement of stock from one owner to another (Shares are transferred upon registration of stock to the new owner and payment of the market value of those shares.)

conversion: the process of moving assigned stock from the seller of a call option or to the seller of a put option (Ownership is converted through the buyer's exercise of the option.)

called away: the result of having stock assigned (For each call option exercised, 100 shares of the seller's stock are called away at the striking price.)

When a buyer decides to exercise, 100 shares of stock are either purchased (called from) or sold (put to) the buyer. The process of calling and putting stock upon exercise is called *conversion*. The stock is assigned at the time of exercise. When a call option is assigned, the stock is said to be *called away*.

Is exercise always a negative to the seller? The answer depends on his or her purpose in having taken a short position. Most option sellers prefer to avoid exercise by either closing the position or by selecting options they believe will be worthless by expiration date. Of course, a seller must also acknowledge that exercise can occur at any time. A buyer has the right to exercise the option far in advance of expiration date, if he or she chooses to do so. This action is called *early exercise*.

In addition, *automatic exercise* is an action that can be taken by the OCC at an option's point of expiration. Remember that the options exchange acts as seller to every buyer and as buyer to every seller. It will match up exercise on the buyer's side against an open seller's position whenever possible. But if, at the time of expiration, there is an excess of sellers, in-the-money options will be exercised automatically.

The decision to avoid exercise is made on the basis of current market value. As long as the option is out of the money, there is no danger of exercise. Once the option goes in the money, the seller has to decide whether to take action to avoid exercise or to allow exercise to occur.

Example: You own 100 shares of stock that originally cost $37 per share. When the value of that stock rose to $42, you sold a call with a striking price of $40 and received a premium of 6 ($600). If exercised, your total profit will be $900 before commissions, consisting of 3 points per share (the difference between the striking price of the option and your original cost) and the option premium you received.

Striking price	$40
Your cost per share	37
Profit	$3
Plus option premium	6
Total profit	$9

In this example, it's possible that you sold the in-the-money call, hoping for exercise. This is one way to sell your stock *and* receive additional income (from the option premium). At the same time, you protect profits already realized. In the event the price of the stock falls, you have received $600 for selling the option. So if the value of the underlying stock falls by six points, you have covered that loss.

Example: You have sold a put with a striking price of $25 per share. The current market value of the stock is $22. You decide to take no action even though if exercised, you will pay $25 per share, which you consider a fair price for the stock. And if the price of the stock increases to $25 per share or more by expiration, the option will not be exercised.

Example: You own 100 shares with a current market value of $29 per share. You sell a call and receive a premium of 4 ($400). The value of the stock falls to $25 per share. Your net basis in the stock has not changed since the amount you

early exercise: the act of exercising an option prior to expiration date (Buyers have the right to exercise at any time.)

automatic exercise: action taken by the Options Clearing Corporation at the time of expiration, when an in-the-money option has not been otherwise exercised or canceled

current market value: the market value of stock at the present time

parity: the condition of an option when the total premium is identical to intrinsic value and no time value exists

received for the option premium is equal to the drop in the stock's value.

The decision to act or wait often is determined by the amount of time value in the option premium. For the buyer, time value is generally a negative factor. You pay an amount above intrinsic value—the difference between *current market value* and striking price—knowing that the intrinsic value will disappear by the time of expiration. But as a seller, time value is potential profit. The greater the time value when you sell, the better is the chance for profit, *because* intrinsic value will disappear between now and expiration date.

Example: You want to buy a call with a striking price of $40. The underlying stock's current market value is $41, and the option premium is 4 (400). You will be paying $300 for time value. If the value of the stock does not change by expiration date, you will lose the time value. So the stock must increase by at least 3 points for you to break even and by more for you to realize a profit.

Example: You plan to sell the same call. The time value of $300 is an advantage for you as long as the stock does not increase in value any more than 3 points. By expiration, that entire time value will go out of the option premium; as long as the stock's value remains within that 3 point limit, you will realize a profit (before brokerage commission).

By the point of expiration, all of the time value will have disappeared from the option's premium. At that point, the option is said to be at *parity*—That is, it consists entirely of intrinsic value.

Using the Daily Options Listings

Keeping in mind that expiration is constantly pending, both buyers and sellers of options must track their open positions. The opportunity for profit or the threat of loss can occur within a very short period of time.

An investor who buys stock can take a more leisurely approach. If you intend to hold that stock for many years, daily price movement will not be as critical to the value of your investment, and the consequences of missing an opportunity will not be as expensive.

You can estimate the value of your options by simply watching daily closing prices of the underlying stock.

Example: You have purchased a call with a striking price of $40 per share, paying a premium of 3 ($300). You intend to sell if and when the option's value goes to 5 or more. By reading the financial page each day, you can track movement of the stock and decide when the time is right to make your move.

To select options to buy or sell or to track results in more detail, you will need to see daily option listings. The *Wall Street Journal* reports daily closing values of all listed options, and *Barron's* reports the same information weekly. Other local papers report option closing prices, but often in an abbreviated or partial format.

Figure 2–2 shows a typical daily option listing. The first column identifies the underlying stock and its current price. In this example, Delta Airlines closed at $37 per share. The second column reports the striking prices of all available options. As a general rule, stocks valued at $100 or less have options available at $5 striking price intervals; above $100, the usual interval is $10.

Columns three through five show current premiums for calls, and columns six through eight are put premiums. Delta Airlines has options on the January, April, July, and October cycle, so three different expiration dates are shown (options only exist for nine months, so the month in the cycle that is farthest away will not be shown; in this example, the October column will appear only after the January options have expired). Notice that the options with the greatest amount of time until expiration have higher time values than those that will expire sooner.

In this example, Delta's current market value is $37 per share. So the $35 calls are $2 in the money. The January contracts reflect time value of only ⅝ of a point. Time value in the longer term options is greater. And the $30 option has 7 points of time value. On the put side, the $40 contract is $3 in the money, and current premium values reflect intrinsic value of at least that much.

		CALLS			PUTS		
		JAN	APR	JUL	JAN	APR	JUL
Delta	25	12	14	17 ½	¹⁄₁₆	s	s
37	30	7 ½	8 ⅜	9	r	⅛	r
37	35	2 ⅝	5 ⅛	7	⅜	2	3 ½
37	40	⅛	1 ½	r	3 ¼	5	r
37	45	r	r	s	8 ½	11	14 ⅛

r – no trades this date
s – not offered

FIGURE 2–2. Example Daily Option Listing

Making an Evaluation

An option buyer's evaluation of an option's listing will involve judgements about:

- Recent volatility and volume in the underlying stock
- Time until expiration of specific option contracts
- The amount of intrinsic and time value
- Current premium levels

Example: You are considering buying a Delta Airlines call. The stock is selling at $37 per share. You will probably eliminate the calls with $25 and $30 striking prices as being too expensive. And the $45 striking price is still 8 points out of the money. The most likely prospects are the calls with either $35 or $40 striking prices.

In this example, the $35 option is 2 points in the money, so you know that the value of the option will change almost dollar for dollar with the underlying stock. If Delta rises by $2 per share, the $35 calls will increase in value by 2 ($200). But if the stock falls to $35 per share, the option will also lose by the same amount.

The January option will expire very soon. If you buy that option, you are paying for very little time value, and from that point of view alone, it is the best bargain for your money. However, with a short expiration, you also take the risk that the option will expire before the stock increases in value. These are offsetting points: low time value versus a short time until expiration. If you buy the January option now and Delta's stock goes up one point, you could make a profit of $100, which is a 38% return. The change in value could occur within a single

day. But you could also lose the entire investment of $262.50 (2 ⅝) if the stock does not in-
crease in value.

You must also consider the commission cost
in an option transaction. If you buy or sell sin-
gle-option contracts, the typical commission will
be $30 to $35, charged both when you buy and
when you sell. So that a rise of 1 point could net
you only $30 after commissions are taken out.

You could also buy the April $35 call, at 5 ⅛
($512.50). The problem here is that you are pay-
ing more than $300 in time value, in exchange
for the extra three months. That time value will
begin to evaporate rapidly as April's expiration
approaches. So the underlying stock will have to
increase at least 3 points during the next three
months, just to break even.

You might also consider the options with $40
striking prices, which is now 3 points out of the
money. You can buy these very cheaply. But
again, you would need a healthy increase in the
stock's value in order to realize a profit before
expiration.

The same process of elimination and risk ap-
praisal can be applied to puts. In order to profit
from buying puts, you must depend on a decline
in the stock's value before expiration—to a degree sufficient to:

- Offset time value premium
- Cover the commission costs of buying and
  selling
- Yield a reasonable profit

If you sell an option, higher time value is a
benefit rather than a disadvantage. But a longer
time period until expiration increases your risks.

For example, look again at the $35 calls. If you
sell the January contract, you have very little
time value, and you're in the money by 2 ⅝
points ($262.50). If the option expires while still
in the money, it will be exercised. If you sell the
April call, you receive more than $300 for time
value, but you are at risk for three months
longer.

Understanding Option Abbreviations

Option values are expressed in daily option listings an abbreviated form. The value of a contract
is always expressed in value per 100 shares. As
shown in Table 2–A, 3 means $300, and 2 ⅝
means $262.50. Options trade down to fractional
values as small as sixteenths of a point, with
each sixteenth being equal to $6.25.

The abbreviated expression of options and
their terms go beyond the current premium.
Both the expiration month and the striking price
are expressed in a shortened version as well. For
example, an October option with a striking price
of $35 per share is called an OCT 35 option.

TABLE 2–A Fractional Values

Fraction	Dollar Value	Fraction	Dollar Value
1/16	$6.25	9/16	$56.25
1/8	12.50	5/8	62.50
3/16	18.75	11/16	68.75
1/4	25.00	3/4	75.00
5/16	31.25	13/16	81.25
3/8	37.50	7/8	87.50
7/16	43.75	15/16	93.75
1/2	50.00	1	100.00

And a January option with a $50 striking price is a JAN 50. Like the premium value, the striking price is expressed without dollar signs.

A complete option description is shown in Figure 2–3. In this example, all of the terms, plus the current premium, are shown. Collectively, the terms distinguish a particular option from all other options.

When you call a broker to make an option trade, you can give directions without using abbreviations. But the broker must translate your instructions to place the order, which could result in an error. Brokers and option customers use a series of symbols to identify the expiration month and the striking price. Figure 2–4 summarizes the symbols that are used by virtually all brokerage firms that trade options for their customers.

The expiration month is always given first, followed immediately by the striking price. Note that the symbol for striking prices of 5, 105, and 205 are identical. One symbol is used for all three, since the daily price of the underlying stock dictates which of the three prices applies.

the complete description

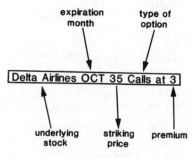

FIGURE 2–3. A Complete Option Description

expiration month symbols		
MONTH	CALLS	PUTS
January	A	M
February	B	N
March	C	O
April	D	P
May	E	Q
June	F	R
July	G	S
August	H	T
September	I	U
October	J	V
November	K	W
December	L	X

striking price symbols			
STRIKING PRICE			SYMBOL
5	105	205	A
10	110	210	B
15	115	215	C
20	120	220	D
25	125	225	E
30	130	230	F
35	135	235	G
40	140	240	H
45	145	245	I
50	150	250	J
55	155	255	K
60	160	260	L
65	165	265	M
70	170	270	N
75	175	275	O
80	180	280	P
85	185	285	Q
90	190	290	R
95	195	295	S
100	200	300	T
7½	–	–	U
12½	–	–	V
17½	–	–	W
22½	–	–	X

FIGURE 2–4. Option Trading Symbols

An example of a specific option: You want to trade a Delta Airlines call with an October expiration and a striking price of $35. The symbol (from Figure 2–4) consists of "J" for the expiration month and "G" for the striking price. If the option is a put, the symbol for expiration month is different.

The option quote also includes an abbreviated symbol for the underlying stock. Every listed stock has its own unique code. Delta Airlines, for example, is described as DAL. So a Delta Airlines call with a striking price of $35 per share, expiring next October, consists of five digits. As illustrated in Figure 2–5, the stock code is listed first, followed by a period and the two-letter code identifying the month and the striking price.

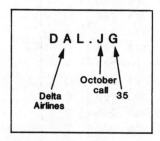

FIGURE 2–5. Example Option Quote

SETTING STANDARDS

Before entering any option trade, you should set standards for yourself. At what point will you close the position, if at all, and what rate of return will you consider acceptable? Or, in the case of sellers, at what level will you close a position and take a loss?

Example: You buy an option at 3 that expires in seven months. You accept the risk that the

underlying stock will not go in the money suffi-
ciently to yield a profit. (In other words, you are
willing to risk losing $300 in exchange for the
potential for gain.) You decide that if the option
increases in value to 5 or more, you will sell.

Example: You own 100 shares of stock and
sell a call with a striking price of $45, receiving
a premium of 4 ($400). You realize that if the
option is exercised, your stock will be called
away. You are willing to accept that risk. However, you also consider the $400 premium an ac-
ceptable level of profit. You set a standard for
yourself: If the value of the option declines to
less than 2, you will close the position by buying the option.

What happens if you don't set a standard?
You might fall into a pattern in which you can
never win. This is the typical experience of people who should not trade options, because they
are unable to resist current trends. Rather than
operating from a firm standard, they react to
what appears to be happening from day to day.

Example: You buy a put (hoping the stock will
fall in value) and pay a premium of 2 ($200).
You hope to double your money, which means
the stock will have to fall at least 2 points. A
few weeks later, the stock has fallen 3 points.
But you do not sell, because you think the stock
might fall even more. But during the next week,
the stock rebounds and rises 2 points. Now, you
realize you should have sold when you had a
profit. So you decide that if it falls again, you
will sell.
Two weeks later, the stock falls to its lowest
level yet, down 4 points. You know you should
sell, but you again wonder if the stock will fall

even more. You hesitate. The stock rebounds. The pattern repeats itself. This process continues until expiration, when your option expires worthless.

You can set and enforce your own standards with the use of *stop orders*, which are contingent orders you can place with your broker.

Example: You buy a call for 4 ($400) and place a stop order for 3. If the value falls to 3 or below, a sale will be executed automatically as soon as possible. There is no guarantee that the order will go through at 3. The trade will be executed as soon as possible, but if the price is falling rapidly, the actual sale price could be well below your target price.

A stop-limit order is more specific and limits losses. Using the same example, a stop-limit order tells the floor broker that the transaction must occur at that price. So if the option is worth 3, it will be executed, but if the option has already fallen below that level, the stop-limit order prevents the sale.

Stop orders can be entered for either buy or sell transactions and can be very useful in enforcing your standards—both for taking profits and for limiting losses.

A word of caution: Not all exchanges allow the use of stop orders for option trading. Before deciding to employ the stop order as part of your strategy, check with your broker and make sure that stop orders are allowed.

Many investors have experimented in the options market and have failed. Why? Because they did not appreciate the absolute necessity for setting a standard and sticking with it.

CALCULATING RATE OF RETURN FOR SELLERS

When you sell options, the rate of return you can expect depends on whether the following conditions apply:

1. You own 100 shares of the underlying stock for each option you sell.
2. The option is exercised.
3. You close the position after favorable decline in premium value.
4. The stock price changes significantly.

The rate of return should always be compared on an annualized basis. If you make a 12 percent profit in two investments, but you hold one for three months and the other for two years, the annual return is substantially different. To annualize a rate of return, you divide the percentage by the number of months held and then multiply the result by 12. For example, the annual return on a 12 percent profit earned in three months is

$$12\% \div 3 = 4.00\%$$
$$4.00\% \times 12 = 48.00\% \text{ annual return}$$

The annual return on 12 percent profit earned in two years is

$$12\% \div 24 = 0.50\%$$
$$0.50\% \times 12 = 6.00\% \text{ annual return}$$

To evaluate the potential return from selling an option, there are two comparative estimates

return if exercised: the estimated rate of return an option seller will earn in the event of exercise (The calculation includes profit on the purchase and sale of the underlying stock, dividends, and premium received.)

return if unchanged: the estimated rate of return an option seller will earn if the option is not exercised (The assumption is that the stock will remain out of the money until expiration, so that the return will consist of the call premium and any dividends earned on the underlying stock.)

of the rate of return: if exercised and if unchanged.

Return if exercised is what you will earn if the underlying stock will be called away. And *return if unchanged* is what you will earn if the option is not exercised. Total income from all sources (gain on the stock, if any, plus dividends and call premium) is divided by the original investment to compute the actual return.

In computing actual return, you must allow for the commissions paid at purchase and at sale. The amount of commission varies by broker and also depends on the number of options involved in a single trade. The more contracts, the lower is the rate of commission.

Example: You own 100 shares of stock that originally cost $38 per share. It is currently valued at $43. You sell a call with a striking price of $40, and receive a premium of 7 ($700). Between now and expiration, you will receive two dividend payments totaling $68.

Return If Exercised

Striking price	$4000
Original cost	3800
Profit	$200
Plus dividends	68
Plus call premium	700
Total profit	$968
Return if exercised ($968 ÷ $3800)	25.47%

Return If Unchanged

Call premium	$700
Plus dividend	68
Total profit	$768
Return if unchanged ($768 ÷ $3800)	20.21%

The next step is to annualize the return. For example, if the time between your purchase of the stock and expiration of the option is nine months, the return if exercised is

25.47% ÷ 9 = 2.83%
2.83% × 12 = 33.96% annual return

and the return if unchanged is

20.21% ÷ 9 = 2.25%
2.25% × 12 = 27.00% annual return

In computing the return if exercised, the calculation involves an offsetting profit and loss if the striking price of the option is lower than the original price you paid for the underlying stock.

Example: You originally purchased 100 shares of stock for $27 per share. You sell a call with a striking price of $25 per share, and receive a premium of 6. You also receive $40 in dividends.

Return if Exercised	
Striking price	$2500
Original cost	2700
Loss	$(200)
Plus dividend	40
Plus call premium	600
Net profit	$440
Return if exercised ($440 ÷ $2700)	16.30%

As an aware options trader, you must calculate the risks in advance of making a trade and set standards you will follow. These standards identify the desired level of profit you hope to achieve and also limit the amount of loss you are willing to accept. Any options investor who experiences an unexpected loss has simply failed to evaluate the ramifications of a particular trade.

Success in the options market means entering an open position with complete awareness of what can happen. You must know when you will cancel a position with an offsetting closing transaction, when to exercise or what will happen if your option is exercised, and what happens upon expiration. You should always have complete knowledge about an investment before you make a decision. But knowledge of profit potential is not enough. You must also be fully aware of the risks that are involved.

3

Buying Calls

___

As a call buyer, you have a choice to make in
the future. You have the right to buy 100 shares
of the underlying stock at the fixed striking
price. And if you choose to exercise that right,
you must do so before the stated expiration date.

That choice is important. You are never obligated to buy the 100 shares; you only hold the
right. Your decision will depend on:

- The actual movement of the underlying
  stock and the subsequent value of the option
- Your reason for buying the call in the first
  place

UNDERSTANDING THE LIMITED LIFE
OF THE CALL

You can become a call buyer purely in the interest of making a profit within a limited amount of

speculation: a risky use of money to create immediate or short-term profits, with the knowledge that substantial or total losses are also likely (Buying calls for leverage is a form of speculation: The buyer might earn a large profit in a short period of time or lose the entire premium.)

suitability: a standard by which an investment or market strategy is judged (The investor's knowledge and experience in options is an important suitability standard, and a strategy is appropriate only if the investor can afford the risks that are involved.)

time. That profit can be made by selling the call at a higher price than you paid for it or by exercising to buy stock below the market value or to offset losses in a short position in the underlying stock. These uses of calls are explained later in this chapter.

You must understand your risks as a buyer before entering this market. Since the calls you purchase will exist for only a limited number of months, you must achieve your purpose as an investor before expiration. Otherwise, you stand to lose the entire premium.

Anyone who has purchased shares of stock knows that time is a luxury. You can hold onto your shares for a day, a week, or for many years. The decision is yours when to sell. Many people buy shares of stock for future appreciation or regular dividend payments over time. Call buyers do not enjoy these privileges. For them, time is not a luxury.

A simple comparison between investing in stock and purchasing a call option puts call options strictly in the arena of *speculation*. Because they are rights and not tangible properties and because their existence is limited by time, the call is nothing more than a side bet. A buyer bets that the market will rise, while a seller bets that the market will fall. Fast—and significant—profits or losses can and do occur for call buyers, and knowing the extent of those profits or losses is an important first step.

To judge the *suitability* of investing in calls, you must comprehend the risks involved and be able to afford taking those chances. You should always know the risks of any investment you make before entering it and be financially able to stand the losses that might occur.

Example: An individual has virtually no experience as an investor and has only $1000 to invest. He wants to increase this fund as quickly as possible, so he decides to buy calls. Although he really cannot afford to lose the money, knowing he might need it by next September when a debt will be payable, he buys three calls for 3 ($300) each. If the stock goes up 3 points or more, he will double his money.

Buying calls is not a suitable investment in this case. The investor cannot afford the losses, and only one possibility has been considered: What happens if the value of the underlying stock goes up. If he is wrong, he stands to lose the entire $1000. The underlying stock might be a solid, secure company with great future potential. But the call buyer depends strictly on timing. If the purchase is made at the wrong time, those profits will not be realized by expiration date.

Example: Another individual has several thousand dollars available and already owns stock and mutual fund shares. She believes these are long-term and fairly secure investments and now wants to devote a small portion of her total portfolio to speculation. She decides to buy three calls and limits her call buying activity to $1000.

As long as this individual understands the risks of buying a call, it can be a suitable way to speculate. If she knows that time works against the call buyer and that timing of the purchase can make the difference between profit and loss, she will be making an informed decision. She is also prepared for the loss and can afford it.

Suitability in the options market refers both to

your ability to take losses and to your knowledge about the risks of this market.

JUDGING THE CALL

Most call buyers lose money. Even when the underlying stock does increase in value, that increase is often not substantial enough to offset the decline in time value.

Example: You purchase a call at 4 ($400) when it is at the money. By expiration, the stock has risen 2 points. Because time value has declined to zero, the call is worth only 2, which is its intrinsic value.

Example: You purchase a call at ⅜ ($37.50) when the stock is 7 points below striking price. By expiration date, the stock has risen 6 points. But the call is nearly worthless at expiration since it is still out of the money.

Calls buyers will lose money if they fail to set goals for themselves: If the premium value falls below their original cost, they do not close the position, hoping to recapture their original cost before expiration; if the value of the stock rises, they hesitate, hoping for yet more profits before expiration. The successful call buyer sets limits and goals and lives by them.

Example: You purchase a call at 4 and establish the following rule for yourself: If the value of the call falls to 2, you will sell and accept a $200 loss. And if the value rises to 7, you will sell and take a profit of $300. If you follow your own rules, you will limit your losses, and you will be able to take your profits when they occur. But because time is limited, you will rarely have a second chance.

Realized profits occur only if profits that can be earned are taken. You must decide at what point you will sell before actually buying a call, and you must stick to that rule. Otherwise, you will earn *paper profits*, but end up with actual losses.

Most call buyers study four attributes: current premium value, the portion of that premium that represents time value, months until expiration, and their own perception of the company. For example, you might look through the listings in the *Wall Street Journal*, seeking a call that is available for a premium of 2 or less, that is at the money or close to it, that has at least three months until expiration, and that is available on a company you consider a strong prospect for growth. This method is flawed. The smallest premiums do not necessarily equal the greatest values.

The best premium values for options with the longest time until expiration are those that are the greatest number of points out of the money. If the striking price is 40, and the stock is now worth less than $35 per share, you can probably buy a call with six months until expiration for a very low price. Of course, you also need that stock to increase far enough in value so that the option will have intrinsic value greater than your cost at the point of expiration. Or the total premium must be greater than your cost at some point before expiration.

Example: You buy a call with a striking price of 40 for a premium of 1 ($100). Expiration is seven months away. The stock is currently sell-

realized profit or loss: profits or losses that are taken when an investor closes a position

paper profits or loss (also called unrealized profits or losses): values that exist only because the current market value is higher or lower than the investor's basis (These profits or losses can be realized—taken— only by closing the position.)

deep in/deep out: terms describing an option when the underlying stock is more than 5 points above or 5 points below the striking price

ing at $34 per share, meaning you are 6 points out of the money. By the expiration date, the stock must be selling above $41 per share in order for you to realize a profit.

Profits are possible in this situation without the stock's value even going in the money. If the stock increases several points shortly after you purchase the call, the premium value might go up one or two points. You can then sell the call and take a profit.

The deeper out of the money, the lower is the cost of the call—and the greater the risk that you will never realize a profit. As shown in Figure 3–1,

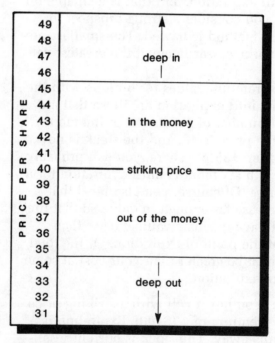

FIGURE 3–1. Deep In/Deep Out Stock Prices

whenever the stock is more than 5 points below the striking price, it is said to be *deep out* of the money. And if the stock is more than 5 points above the striking price, it is *deep in* the money.

ESTABLISHING GOALS

Most people think of buying options as a purely speculative activity. If the price goes up, you make a profit, and if it goes down, you lose. While that is a basic fact about the speculative nature of simply buying calls to make a profit, they can also be used for more conservative reasons.

Goal 1: Gaining Leverage

Leverage is the most common reason for buying calls—that is, they create the potential for substantial gain with a limited amount of money. To show how quickly such profits (or losses) can occur, let's assume that you are comparing risks between the purchase of 100 shares of stock and a call that will expire in four months. See Figure 3–2.

The stock is selling at $62 per share. You may either buy 100 shares, which will cost $6200, or you can purchase a call with a striking price of 60 for a more limited investment of 5 ($500). Of the total premium, 2 points represent intrinsic value and 3 points are time value.

If you buy 100 shares of the stock, you must pay for your purchase within five business days. If you buy a call, you must make payment on the business day following the transaction. These payment deadlines are the *settlement dates*.

leverage: the use of a limited amount of money to control greater values (A call buyer who spends $300 to control $5000 worth of stock has more leverage than an investor who spends $5000 to buy 100 shares.)

settlement date: the date on which an investor must pay for purchases or is paid for sales (Stock settlement occurs five business days after the transaction date; option settlement occurs on the business day following the transaction.)

rate of return

	STOCK (1)		CALL (2)	
	PROFIT OR LOSS	RATE OF RETURN	PROFIT OR LOSS	RATE OF RETURN
price increase of 5 points	$500	8.1%	$500	100%
price increase of 1 point	$100	1.6%	$100	20%
no price change	0	0	0	0
price decrease of 1 point	–$100	–1.6%	–$100	–20%
price decrease of 5 points	–$500	–8.1%	–$500	–100%

(1) purchased at $62 per share ($6,200)

(2) striking price 60, premium 5 ($500)

FIGURE 3–2. Rate of Return: Buying Stocks versus Calls

As a call buyer, your plan is to sell the option before expiration. Like most call buyers, you have no intention of exercising the option, but are hoping for enough of an increase in value to make a profit before expiration.

For $500, you have control over 100 shares of stock. That's leverage. You do not need to invest $6200 to have that control. Without considering the commission cost of buying and selling the option, what could happen in the immediate future?

If the stock rises 5 points, the stockholder's $500 profit represents an 8.1% return, but the call buyer will realize a 100% return: the 5 points of profit on a $500 investment. The profit will occur only if the increase in the call's value occurs rather quickly. The longer it takes for this profit to occur, the more deterioration will occur from reduced time value. If the stock has increased at the point of expiration to $67 per share, the option will be worth 7, rather than 10, and the 3 points of time value will be gone.

An increase of 1 point in value yields 1.6% to the stockholder, but 20% to the option buyer. If there is no price change, you will be able to sell your call for the same price you paid (less commissions)—again, assuming you sell the option *before* time value declines. If you wait too long, the premium will diminish between purchase and expiration dates. For example, if the stock stays at $62 per share, your option (originally costing you 5) will decline in value to 2 at the expiration date.

As a call buyer, you are under the pressure of time for two reasons. First, the option will expire at a specified date in the future. And second, as you approach expiration, time value declines. This is why the chances of loss are high for buyers. An increase in value of the underlying stock is not enough. That increase must yield a profit above and beyond the time value in the premium you pay.

You can buy calls that have little or no time value. But to do so, you must select calls that are close to expiration, which means you have only a short time for the stock to increase in value.

Example: In the second week of May, the May 50 call on an underlying stock is selling for 2, and the stock is worth 51 ⅝ (1 ⅝ points in the money). You buy one call. By the third Friday (next week), you hope for an increase in the underlying stock's value. If the stock goes up by 1 point, the option will be profitable.

Because time is short, your chances of realizing a profit are limited. But profits—if they do occur—will be close to dollar for dollar with movement in the stock. If that stock jumps 3 points, you could double your money in a few days. If it declines by 2 points, you will lose all or most of your premium.

The more time until expiration, the greater is the time value premium—and the more increase you need in the underlying stock just to maintain value. See Figure 3–3.

diminishing time value

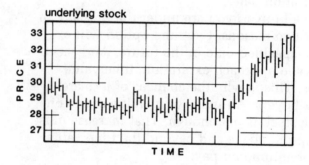

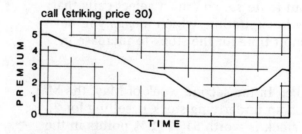

FIGURE 3–3. Diminishing Time Value of the Call Relative to the Underlying Stock

Example: You buy an option for 5 when the stock is at or near the striking price. The advantage is that you have eight months until expiration. The underlying stock remains fairly close to the striking price until the last two months, when it moves up to $33 per share. But because all of the time value has disappeared, your option is only worth 3, and you have lost $200.

Buying calls for leverage (controlling 100 shares of stock for a small amount of money) offers the potential for substantial gain. But because of time value and the ever-pending expiration, the risks are also great. Even with the best timing and analysis, it is extremely difficult to consistently earn profits by buying calls and hoping for timely price increases.

Goal 2: Limiting Risks

In one respect, the limited amount of money you put into buying a call *reduces* your risks. A stockholder's losses are greater when a stock falls many points.

Example: You buy an option for a premium of 3. The stock falls 17 points by expiration date. As a call buyer, you will lose your premium of $300, but stockholders have lost $1700. The stockholders enjoy the luxury of being able to hold onto those shares indefinitely, hoping the market value will eventually rebound. But for the moment, the value of their investment is much lower than when they purchased.

The time factor impedes the value of limiting risks. You benefit only as long as the option exists, with expiration a reality you cannot escape. The stockholder has money more at stake, but is not concerned with expiration dates.

It would make no sense to buy calls *only* to limit risks. That's a side benefit to leverage. You must assume that if you buy a call, it is in the expectation of rising stock prices in the immediate future. But in the event you are wrong, your losses are limited to the amount you risk in premium.

Goal 3: Planning Future Purchases

When you own a call, you fix the price of a future purchase in the event you do decide to exercise. This use of calls goes beyond pure speculation.

Example: The market recently experienced a severe drop in value. You have been following the stock of one company, which previously was trading in a range between $50 and $60 per share. After the drop, that stock is valued at $39. You would like to buy 100 shares at today's depressed value. Your belief is that when the market does turn around, the stock will prove to be a bargain at its current price, but you do not have the $3900 to buy 100 shares. You will receive enough cash to make your purchase in about six months, but you don't want to miss the opportunity to buy 100 shares now.

To fix the price, you can buy a call while market values are low, with the intention of exercising that call when you do have the money. The 40 call is selling for 3, and you purchase one contract at that price. Six months later, the stock has increased to $58 per share. The option is worth 18 just before its expiration date.

You have a choice. You can either sell your call for 18, realizing a profit of $1500 (18 less your cost of 3). Or you can exercise the call and buy 100 shares at $40 per share. If you are seeking long-term growth and prefer the permanent value of owning stock, this is one way to use options—that is, to buy a call when you consider stock prices a bargain and later to exercise to purchase stock at below-market prices.

If you were wrong and the value of the stock does not increase, you lose the premium you invested. But you also avoid the risk of buying stock that did not increase in value as you had expected.

Goal 4: Insuring Profits

A final reason to buy calls is to protect a short position in the underlying stock. Most investors buy stocks hoping values will rise in the future. At some point, they mean to sell those shares and realize a profit. Other investors believe values will fall, and they sell shares, taking a short position. If they are right, values will decline, and their short positions can be closed out at a profit.

Example: An investor sells short 100 shares when market value is $58 per share. A month later, the stock's value has fallen to $52. He makes a closing purchase transaction—buying 100 shares—and realizes a profit of $600.

A short seller's risks are virtually unlimited. If he is wrong and values increase, he can close a position only by buying 100 shares at a higher price than the market value at the time the short sale was made. To protect themselves against this risk, short sellers often buy calls.

Example: An investor sells short 100 shares when market value is $58 per share. At the same time, she buys one call with a striking price of $65 for a premium of ⅞ ($87.50). Her risk is no longer unlimited. If market value rises above $65 per share, the value of the call protects the position. Risk is limited to 7 points (between her short sale price of $58 and the call's striking price of $65).

In this case, a deep-out-of-the-money call is fairly inexpensive, yet it provides a form of insurance to the short seller. Of course, this protection is good only as long as the call exists. So the short seller must either decide to exercise the call before expiration or replace it with another call before expiration.

The short seller reduces and limits risk, but also reduces the likely profit by buying calls. The premium paid for that protection can be expensive if the value of calls is too high.

Example: A short seller must pay a premium of 2 for the call he needs over the next eight months. If the value of the stock declines by 2 points, he would normally be able to realize a $200 profit. But because he also paid for insurance in the form of a call, he will have only broken even at that point.

Profit in the short sale	$200
Loss in the call purchase	(200)
Profit	$0

Calls serve an important function when used by short sellers to limit risks. But they also take part of the profit away from the short selling strategy. In the event the stock does fall in value, the short seller will absorb the premium cost. But if stock values do climb, having the protection of the call can save thousands of dollars.

DEFINING PROFIT ZONES

Whatever strategy you employ in your portfolio, you should always be aware of what is required to create a profit and to what ranges of potential loss you expose yourself. You need to know the break-even price of your investment, as well as the profit and loss zones. See Figure 3–4.

Example: You buy a call at a premium of 3, with a striking price of 50. What must the stock's price be by the point of expiration to break even? What price must the stock achieve to create a profit? And at what price will you suffer a loss?

A loss occurs if the option expires out of the money (below the striking price). Because you paid a premium of 3, when the price is 3 points or less above striking price, you will suffer a limited loss. That is, if at the point of expiration, the stock is worth $52 per share, you can sell your call for 2 and take a loss of $100. If the

break-even price (also called break-even point): the price of the underlying stock at which the option investor breaks even (For the call buyer, this price amounts to the number of points above the striking price of the stock that equals the price of the call before allowing for commission costs.)

profit zone: the price range of the underlying stock in which the option investor will realize a profit (For a call buyer, the profit zone extends upward from the break-even price.)

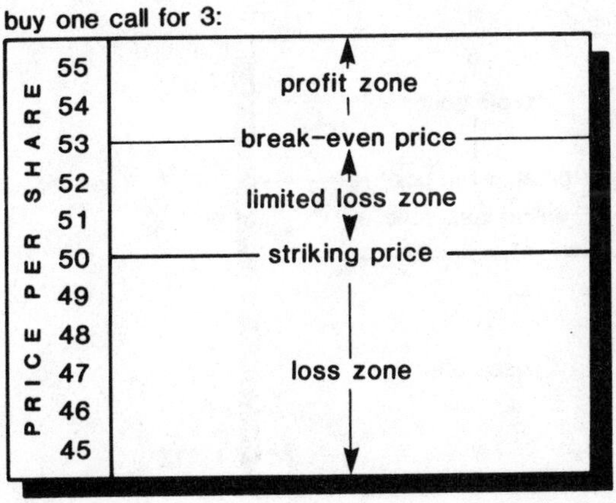

buy one call for 3:

FIGURE 3–4. A Call's Profit and Loss Zone

loss zone: the
price range of the
underlying stock in
which the option
investor will lose
(A limited loss oc-
curs for a call
buyer between the
striking price and
the break-even
price; otherwise,
the loss zone is any
stock price lower
than the option's
striking price.)

stock's value is at $53 per share, you are at the break-even point (without considering commission costs). And if the stock's price is above that level, you are in the profit zone.

Defining profit and loss zones and the break-even price helps you develop a goal for yourself when considering a call purchase. You must be willing to limit losses when stock values decline rather than rise and to take profits when they occur.

An example of a *call purchase*, with defined profit and loss zones, is shown in Figure 3–5. In this example, you buy one May 40 call for 2 (−$200). In order to profit from this strategy, the call's value must increase to a point greater than the striking price *and* the cost of the option. In this case, you invested $200. So $42 per share is your break-even point. Time value will deteriorate between the purchase date and expiration, so that increases must occur rapidly or they must consist of intrinsic value.

Clearly identifying the ranges for limiting

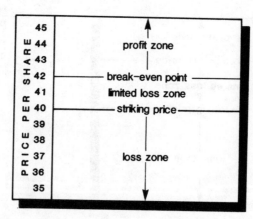

FIGURE 3–5. Example Call Purchase

losses and for taking profits if you employ the advanced strategies of buying and selling options that are described in later chapters. But even for buying a call that will expire within a few months, you should know in advance what risks you take and how much price movement will be needed to yield a profit.

Example: You are considering buying a call for a premium of 2, with a striking price of $35. The stock is now worth $33 per share, so the entire premium is time value. In defining your profit and loss zones and identifying a break-even price, you realize the stock must increase by 4 points or more. You conclude that the risk is too great for the $200, and you decide not to make the purchase.

Example: You have been following price movement of a stock on which options are available. One option has a current premium of 1 and is at the money; the expiration date comes up in three months. Your break-even price is only 1 point away. You consider this investment a worthwhile risk for $100, especially since the stock, in your opinion, is likely to increase in value before expiration.

Before buying calls, you must evaluate the underlying stock's value now and in relation to its recent price range. You also need to judge the total market. Do you believe prices will rise or fall? And how responsive is the underlying stock to general movement of the market? The history of the stock's volatility should always be considered when you are thinking of buying a call. See Chapter Six for a more expanded description of stock selection.

Beyond that analysis, you must be willing to live with the time factor. Your call will expire within a few months, meaning value must accumulate within a limited period of time. And any time value must be more than offset in the stock's increasing price in order to yield a profit.

In the next chapter, strategies for buying puts will be examined and explained in depth.

4

Buying Puts

If you buy puts, you own the right to sell 100 shares of the underlying stock at a fixed striking price by the exercise date. This choice is opposite of the choice a call buyer makes (the right to buy 100 shares under the same terms).

Like the call buyer, you are not obligated to sell the 100 shares. You have the right, but might decide instead to sell the option for a profit. The decision to exercise depends on:

- The movement in the underlying stock and, as a result, the change in the value of the put option
- Your motive for purchasing the put

UNDERSTANDING THE LIMITED LIFE OF THE PUT

Puts can be purchased strictly on speculation. If you believe the underlying stock will be worth less in the near future, you can either sell the stock short or buy a put.

Short selling of stock is a strategy employed by investors who believe the stock's value will fall. If they are correct, they will be able to close the position by buying the stock at a lower price. A short seller borrows the stock from the brokerage firm and then sells it. The brokerage firm demands a deposit of a portion of the stock's market value at the time of the short sale. If the stock's market value rises, the brokerage firm requires that more money be put on account.

The entire amount of the stock's market value is at risk, because the investor must make a deposit and must pay interest to the brokerage firm for the difference between the deposit and the market value. In that respect, selling short requires the same level of investment risk as buying stock.

Selling stock short is a very risky strategy with unlimited risk. A short seller hopes to gain from a price decline. But if the timing is wrong and the stock goes up instead of down, the seller will lose money.

Example: You believe a stock is overpriced and will probably lose value in the future. You instruct your broker to sell short 100 shares. Several weeks later, the stock has fallen by 7 points. You call your broker again and place a closing purchase transaction order to buy the stock for 7 points below the sales price. Your profit (before broker commissions) is $700.

Example: You sell short when the stock is priced at $49 per share (believing the price will continue to fall). A week later, another company announces a tender offer for the company at $65 per share. The stock immediately rises to $63. If you enter a closing purchase transaction at that point, you will lose $1400 (plus broker commissions). If the tender offer is accepted, you will eventually have to take the loss.

Instead of taking the risks of selling short, you can benefit from a stock's decline by buying puts and limit the risk in case your timing is wrong.

The limit of risk is a positive feature of buying puts. However, the put—like all options—will exist for a limited amount of time. If the strategy is to be profitable, price movement in the underlying stock must occur before expiration date. And the movement must be significant enough to surpass the amount you pay in premium. That movement must occur before expiration. So a put buyer trades limited risk for limited life.

Understanding the potential benefits is only half of the equation necessary if you are to succeed as a put buyer. You must also understand the risk and know how much price movement in the underlying stock will be needed to produce a profit.

Too many speculators buy puts with high time value and thus require many points of decline in the stock's value in order to profit. If the stock is fairly stable in its price movement, the chances of profit are greatly reduced.

Buying puts is suitable for you only if you understand these risks and if you are familiar with the price history of the underlying stock. You must also be able and willing to lose the entire put premium.

Example: An investor has $500 to invest, but she thinks the market will fall in the near future. She cannot afford to lose the $500, which represents her entire savings. She buys two puts at a premium of 2, for a total of $400. The market does fall, but the underlying stock is not affected. It declines only 3 points. At expiration date, her puts are worth 1 point each. She sells the two puts and receives $200.

This investor's perception of the market was correct. Prices fell. But the puts were not profitable, because the stock was too stable to produce a profit in a limited period of time. In addition, puts were not appropriate for this individual. She could not afford the loss.

The investor in this example failed to analyze the market and the feasibility of buying puts. She saw only the potential for gain and did not consider the potential for loss. She also ignored the strength of the underlying stock. If it is unlikely to decline in value quickly enough to produce a profit, put buying is a poor idea.

If you understand the risks and can afford to speculate, put buying might have a place in your portfolio.

Example: An experienced investor owns stocks, real estate, and shares of two mutual funds. He considers his portfolio as a long-term one and is not concerned with immediate price movement. He also has several hundred dollars available for speculation and thinks the near-term market will fall. He buys puts with the money, selecting stocks that are most likely to fall enough to produce a profit.

This individual understands the risks involved in speculation, and already has built a base in his portfolio. Diversifying with a portion of his capital is appropriate as long as he understands the risks and is willing and able to lose money. With that risk in mind, he takes the chance, hoping for a short-term profit.

JUDGING THE PUT

Time works against all option buyers. Not only will your option expire in a few months, but you must also accept the declining time value of the put.

You can select a low-priced put—one that is out of the money—and will need many points of price movement for a profit. Or you can select a put that is in the money. In that case, if the stock moves in the wrong direction, you stand to lose more.

Example: You buy a put, paying a premium of 4 ($400) when the stock's value is 3 points below the striking price (in the money). You have six months until expiration. At the point of expiration, the stock has risen 3 ½ points, and your option is worth only ½ ($50). The time value has come out of the option, and only the intrinsic value remains. If you sell at this point, you lose $350.

Example: You buy a put and pay a premium of ½ ($50). The stock's value is 4 points above the striking price (out of the money), and you have six months until expiration. At the point of expiration, the stock has declined 4 ½ points, so it is ½ point in the money. Its value is ½. If you sell at this point, you break even. (Actually, you lose money because you will pay a brokerage commission when you buy and again when you sell.)

The problem is not limited to picking the right direction the underlying stock will move. The degree of movement must be great enough to produce a profit within the limited time before expiration of the put.

Some speculators buy out-of-the-money puts because the premium is relatively low. For a bargain price, though, you need a lot of price movement to earn even a modest profit. In comparison, an in-the-money put will cost more, but to earn a profit, less price movement is required.

Example: You buy an in-the-money put and pay 7 ($700). A week later, the stock falls 1 point. You sell the put and take a $100 profit. That's a 14 percent return in one week.

You need to set goals for yourself whenever you speculate in puts. Do not allow the "greed factor" to take over. Identify in advance when you will sell. That means limiting losses and recognizing what you consider a target gain.

Example: You purchase a put for a premium of 5 and set the following standards: If the value of the put declines to 3 or less, you will sell and take a $200 loss. And if the value rises to 8 or more, you will sell and take a $300 gain. You hope for a 60 percent gain and are willing to risk a 40 percent loss.

Setting goals is the only way to succeed if you plan to speculate in options. Too many speculators fall into the no-win trap because they fail to set standards for themselves.

Example: You purchase a put for 5 and plan to sell if it increases to 7 or more. Within two weeks, the stock falls and the put increases in value to 8—a gain of 3 points. You do not sell, however, thinking the stock might continue to fall. You do not want to lose any future profits. The following week, the stock rebounds, and the put falls again to 5.

The lost opportunity might not repeat, so potential profits are not taken. The same logic applies when a put option loses value.

Example: You purchase a put for 5 and decide to close the position if it declines in value to 3. A month later, the stock rises, and the put falls. You should sell, but you're hoping that the stock will fall and that the put will again climb in value.

Even if the stock does eventually fall, time is still working against you. The longer it takes for the turnaround in value, the more time value you lose. The stock could fall a point or two over a three-month period, in which case you will be trading time value for intrinsic value. You might never get back to an acceptable minimal loss level.

The problem of time value is the same problem that call buyers experience. With puts, a decline in the value of the underlying stock is advantageous. See Figure 4–1.

Example: You buy a put for a premium of 5 ($500) with a striking price of 30. Between purchase date and expiration, the underlying stock rises above the striking price, but then falls to 27, which is 3 points below. If you sell the put at expiration, you will lose $200, because time value has gone out of the put. Even though the stock is 3 points in the money, it was not enough to yield a profit.

The farther out of the money a stock is, the cheaper the premium for a put—and the lower the chance for profit. And the farther in the money a stock is, the more expensive the put, because you will be paying both for time and intrinsic value.

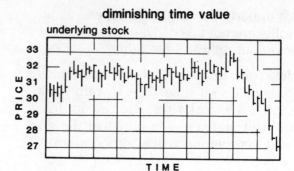

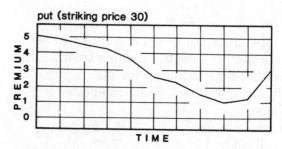

FIGURE 4–1. Diminishing Time Value of the Put Relative to the Underlying Stock

If you buy an in-the-money put and the underlying stock increases in value, you will lose one dollar of premium value for every point of movement. And of course, you gain one dollar for every point of decline.

Whether you prefer lower premium puts that are out of the money or in-the-money puts that cost more, be aware of the number of points between the stock's current value and the striking price. The more points away, the greater your risks.

To minimize this risk, limit your speculation to within 5 points from the striking price. As shown in Figure 4–2, you should avoid deep in and deep out puts, as they will either be too ex-

deep in/deep out

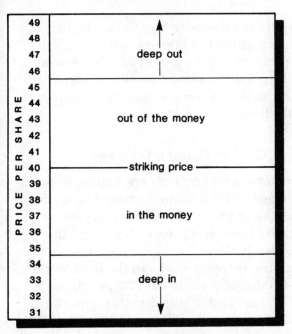

FIGURE 4–2. Deep In/Deep Out Puts

pensive or too far away from a profitable price
level.

Set goals and stay with them. Consider the
premium value, the mix of time and intrinsic
value, the time until expiration, and the price
movement and strength of the underlying stock.
Do not make the most common speculator's mistake: shopping for a put based only on premium
bargains and time until expiration. Look at the
entire picture, and remember that there is an
inescapable relationship between the stock and
the put. Volatility and perceptions of that company by the investing public will determine how
your put will perform between purchase and expiration.

ESTABLISHING GOALS

There are three reasons to buy puts. The first is
purely speculative: the hope of realizing a substantial profit in a short period of time. Second,
you can buy puts to avoid the risks of short selling. Third, puts can serve as a form of insurance
against declines in stock you own.

Goal 1: Gaining Leverage

Most investors who buy puts are hoping to profit
from leverage. With a limited amount of money
available, the potential for profits is greater with
puts than it is in selling stock short. And the
risks are also limited.

Here's how leverage works in the case of puts.
A stock is currently valued at $62 per share. If
you sell it short and it falls 5 points, you can
close the position and realize a $500 gain. If you
believe the stock will fall and instead of selling
it short, you buy 12 puts (total $6000), your po-
tential for profit is greater. A drop of 5 points
will yield a $6000 gain, or a 100 percent return,
assuming that no time value is lost.

If you do not have a lot of capital available to
make the choice between selling stock and buying puts, you can still use leverage to your advantage.

Example: You buy a put for a premium of 5
($500) with a striking price of 60. The stock is
currently selling at $60 per share. Aware of the
risks and the potential rewards of this strategy,
you compare leverage to the potential rewards
and risks of selling short 100 shares. As shown
in Figure 4–3, a drop of 5 points in the stock
would produce a $500 gain, with either strategy.

rate of return

	STOCK (1)		PUT (2)	
	PROFIT OR LOSS	**RATE OF RETURN**	**PROFIT OR LOSS**	**RATE OF RETURN**
price decrease of 5 points	$500	8.1%	$500	100%
price decrease of 1 point	$100	1.6%	$100	20%
no price change	0	0	0	0
price increase of 1 point	–$100	–1.6%	–$100	– 20%
price increase of 5 points	–$500	–8.1%	–$500	–100%

(1) sold short at $62 per share ($6,200)

(2) striking price 60, premium 5 ($500)

FIGURE 4–3. Rates of Return: Selling Short Versus Buying Puts

Because a short sale requires the combination of a deposit of part of the stock's value with the brokerage firm, as well as interest payments on the difference, the short seller is just as committed to the value of the stock as a buyer would be. So any comparison of yields should be based on an understanding that short sellers are at risk for 100 shares of stock.

A decline of 5 points produces an 8.1 percent profit to the short seller and a 100 percent yield to the put buyer. For that difference in yield, compare the risks. The short seller's risks are unlimited; the stock could rise to any level. The put buyer's risk is limited to the $500 paid for the premium. A drop of 1 point in value of the stock will produce a 1.6 percent profit to the

short seller and a 20 percent profit to the put
buyer.

Losses can be compared on a similar basis.
When a short seller's stock rises in value, the
loss can be substantial. But the amount of loss
for the put buyer is limited to the amount paid
for the put.

Most put buyers never intend to exercise the
put. If puts increase in value, the put is sold for
a higher price than its purchase value.

Goal 2: Limiting Risks

It is possible to double your money in a very
short period of time by speculating in puts. And
the leveraging of your money increases even a
modest investment's potential. In one respect, leverage increases risks; in another, it decreases
risks.

Risks are increased with leverage because you
could lose the entire amount invested. The more
you invest in puts, the more you stand to gain—
or to lose.

Example: You buy a put and pay a premium
of 3. But by expiration date, the stock has risen
in value above the striking price. The put expires and you lose the entire $300. Time has
worked against you. The stock might eventually
fall below the striking price, but not necessarily
before expiration of your put.

Risks are decreased when your alternative is
selling short. If a stock rises instead of falling as
you expect, your puts will decline in value. But
if you sell short, you must make up the difference when you close the short position. And
that could be many thousands of dollars more
than you'd planned.

Example: An investor sells short 100 shares of a stock valued at $35 per share. That stock climbs to $44, and the investor, fearing further rises, closes the position. He buys the stock at $44 and loses $900. If the same investor had purchased a put instead of selling short, the potential loss would have been limited to the total of the premium paid, and the fear of further price increases in the stock would not be a factor.

Some investors prefer short selling over buying puts because there is no time pressure involved. A put will expire within nine months, while a short position can be left open indefinitely. As long as the short seller is able to keep the required deposit on account with the brokerage firm, and as long as that investor is willing to pay interest on the difference between the deposit and current market value, the short position does not expire like an option.

The risks of a short position can be reduced by buying calls, as explained in the last chapter. Of course, calls also expire, so to maintain protection of a short position, the investor must be willing to replace one call with another as expiration occurs. Buying calls to protect a short position adds to the cost and requires greater declines in value to produce a profit.

If you believe a stock's value will fall, the alternative of buying puts makes sense. The risk of loss is limited, and your broker will not require that you deposit a large sum of money to cover a short sale.

For the convenience of having leverage, you must be able to accept losses when stock goes up instead of down. You must also be willing to accept the disadvantage of time. Your put will expire in a few months. Every put buyer has the

married put: descriptive of a hedge position when a put and 100 shares are bought at the same time (The put is "married" to the 100 shares on which the downside protection is provided.)

hedge: a strategy in which one position protects the other (Buying a put is a form of hedge to protect the value of 100 shares of the underlying stock.)

put to seller: the action that occurs when a put buyer exercises the put (The 100 shares of stock are sold—put —to the seller at the striking price.)

added disadvantage of time value premium. As expiration nears, that value disappears from the option, even when the stock does not rise in price.

Goal 3: Hedging a Long Position

Put buying is not always purely speculative. A very conservative strategy involves buying one put for every 100 shares of the underlying stock you buy as a way of protecting yourself from declines in price. Each put is known as a *married put* since it is tied to the underlying stock.

The risk of decline in price is a constant concern of every investor. If you buy stock and it falls in value, you might sell, fearing further declines. Or you might hold onto it, hoping for a rebound. It could take months or even years for a stock to recover from a severe decline. For protection against such declines, you buy puts as a form of insurance, which is known as a *hedge* strategy. In the event of a decline in value of the stock, you can exercise the put and sell your stock through exercise. This action is called *put to seller*.

Example: You buy 100 shares of stock at $57 per share. To protect against a decline in price, you also spend $100 to buy a put with a striking price of 50. Two months later, the stock has fallen to $36 per share, and the put is near expiration. The put has a current value of 14 ($1400).

In this situation, you have two choices.

1. Sell the put, and realize a $1300 profit. Your original cost of the investment was $58 per share (purchase price of $57, plus 1 point to buy the put). Your net cost is $45 ($5800 investment, less $1300 profit on the put). Your basis is now 9 points above current market value. If the stock increases in value, you will realize a profit once it exceeds the $45 level. Without the put, your basis would be 21 points above current market value.

2. Exercise the put, and sell the stock for $50 per share. In this instance, you sell for 8 points below your original cost. You will lose the $100 paid for the insurance provided by the put, plus commissions on the stock purchase and upon exercise of the option.

downside protection: a strategy involving the purchase of one put for every 100 shares owned, as a form of insurance (Every point drop in the stock is matched by an increase of 1 point in the put.)

Regardless of the choice you make, you end up better off than if you had simply purchased the stock without the protection of the put. You either cut the amount of loss following a severe decline in the underlying stock's value, or you realize a profit on the put while keeping the stock.

The two choices—exercising or selling the put —both result in losses. Remember, though, that without the put, the loss in the stock would be severe. It's better to lose a little than to lose a lot, and a put can be used to protect your position in a stock to that degree.

Downside protection takes away from your potential for gain. The money invested in the put's premium will reduce future profits in the event the stock rises, but that reduction is limited. Of greater concern should be the limit on the downside.

In the event the stock's value rises, your potential losses are frozen to the amount of the put's premium, and no more. Whether you exercise the put or sell it at a profit, downside protection helps you establish an acceptable level of loss and to fix that loss for the duration of the put's life.

Example: You recently purchased 100 shares of stock at $60 per share. At the same time, you bought a call with a striking price of 60, paying a premium of 3 ($300). The total amount invested is $6300. Before making your purchases, you analyzed the potential profit or loss and concluded that your losses would never exceed 4.8 percent ($300 paid for the put, divided by $6300, the total amount you spent).

You also recognize that an increase in the stock's value of 3 points or less is not a profit at all. Your total basis is $6300 (combining the stock purchase with the call premium). So profits do not begin to accrue until the stock's value exceeds $63 per share.

A summary of this analysis is shown in Figure 4–4. Note that regardless of the severity of decline in the stock's price, the loss never exceeds 4.8 percent of the total amount invested. That's because, for every point the stock falls in value, the option gains a point of intrinsic value.

DEFINING PROFIT ZONES

To decide whether buying a put is a reasonable move to make, always be aware of potential profits and losses. Pay special attention to the number of points the stock must move to produce profits, while also keeping in mind the time you have until expiration.

Comparing limited losses to potential profits when using puts for downside protection is one analysis that will help you determine the value of buying a put. And when trying to pick a

downside protection

PRICE MOVEMENT, UNDERLYING STOCK	PROFIT OR LOSS STOCK (1)	PROFIT OR LOSS PUT (2)	NET PROFIT OR LOSS (3) AMOUNT	NET PROFIT OR LOSS (3) RATE
down 20 points	-$2,000	$1,700	-$ 300	- 4.8%
down 5 points	-$ 500	$ 200	-$ 300	- 4.8%
down 3 points	-$ 300	0	-$ 300	- 4.8%
no change	0	-$ 300	-$ 300	- 4.8%
up 3 points	$ 300	-$ 300	0	0
up 5 points	$ 500	-$ 300	$ 200	3.2%
up 20 points	$2,000	-$ 300	$1,700	27.0%

(1) stock purchased at $60 per share
(2) put striking price 60, premium 3
(3) return based on total cost of $6,300

FIGURE 4–4. Downside Protection: Selling Short versus Buying Puts

sound speculative investment, the time until expiration and the distance between current stock value and the striking price—as well as time value—will help you identify a worthwhile risk.

The profit and loss zones for puts are the reverse of the same zones for a call. When you buy a call, you hope for a rise in the stock's price. But as a put buyer, you will profit if the value of the stock falls. See Figure 4–5.

Example: You buy a put with a striking price of 50 and pay a premium of 3 ($300). Your break-even point is $47 per share. Once the stock falls to that level, it will have intrinsic value equal to the premium you paid. Your put

a put's profit and loss zones

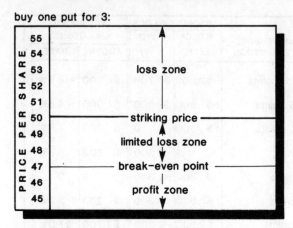

FIGURE 4–5. A Put's Profit and Loss Zones

can be sold between $47 and $50 per share for a limited loss. And if the price goes above the striking price of $50 per share, the put will be worthless at the point of expiration.

Before buying any put, determine the profit, loss, and break-even zones. For the money you will be placing at risk, how much price movement will be needed to yield a profit? How much time will you have? And is the risk worth taking?

An example of a put purchase, with defined profit and loss zones, is shown in Figure 4–6. In this example, you buy one May 40 put for 3 (−$300). The outcome of this strategy is the exact opposite of buying a call. You will profit if the value of stock falls below the striking price of 40. However, the point decline must be greater than your purchase price by expiration; otherwise, the put will be worth less than the $300 invested. Like call purchasing, time works against you when you buy puts. They will ex-

put purchase

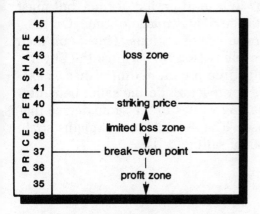

FIGURE 4–6. Example Put Purchase

pire within a short number of months. However, risk is limited to the amount spent on premium.

The mistake most investors make is failing to set any standards for themselves. You should plan to cut your losses at a specific level and to sell your put once you realize an acceptable amount of profit.

Remember the important points to evaluate in buying puts:

- Your motive (leverage, reduction of risk, or downside protection)
- The premium and amount of time value
- Time until expiration
- Distance between the stock's current market value and the striking price
- The number of points needed to yield a profit
- Characteristics of the underlying stock (Chapter Six provides guidelines for selecting stocks appropriate to your option strategy.)

Option buyers stand to earn impressive percentage gains in a short period of time, but must also live with the disadvantage of time. On the other side are sellers of options. Time is on their side for the same reason it is against the buyer: The time value in a premium diminishes as expiration date approaches. So the seller benefits from diminishing values to the same degree that the buyer loses. The next chapter explains strategies and risks of selling calls.

5

Selling Calls

The he most common investment sequence involves buying a security and later selling it.
However, that sequence can be reversed. When
you start out by selling an option, you expect to
later cancel the position by buying the same option at a lower premium.

Sellers have an important advantage over buyers. The time value declines over the life of the
option so that, at the point of expiration, none
remains. So time is on your side as a seller. Unlike the buyer, for whom time value is a problem, the seller wants the highest possible time
value at the point of sale and purchases with the
hope that time value will evaporate.

When you sell a call, you grant the buyer the
right to buy 100 shares of the underlying stock
at the striking price and at any time before expiration.

Most investment strategies contain characteristics of risk that are clearly identified and un-

changing. But selling calls can be extremely
risky or extremely conservative. It is one of the
few strategies that offers extremes at either end
of the risk spectrum.

SELLING UNCOVERED CALLS

If you sell a call when you do not own 100
shares, you are taking a great risk. In fact, this
type of sale is one of the highest forms of risk an
investor can take: a short position with unlimited potential for loss.

Remembering that the short position grants a
buyer the right to buy 100 shares at the striking
price, you must be prepared to deliver those
shares if the call is exercised. If you do not own
those shares, you will be required upon exercise
to buy them at the current market value and
then sell them at the striking price.

Example: The underlying stock is currently
valued at $34 per share. The July 35 call's pre-
mium is 4 ($400). You do not own any shares of
the stock, but you sell a July 35 call. Your brokerage firm will add $400 to your account. Be-
fore expiration, the stock unexpectedly soars to
$61 per share, and your option is exercised. You
will lose $2200 (current market value of $61,
less the striking price of $35, and less the $400
premium you receive).

Current market value	$6100
Less striking price	− 3500
Less call premium	− 400
Loss	$2200

When you do not own 100 shares and a call is
exercised, you are required to deliver and must

therefore buy those shares at the current value. Because market value is determined by demand, the per-share price is potentially unlimited.

Because of this risk, your broker will allow you to sell calls without shares only if you have adequate shares of other stocks, cash, or other value in your account that serve as protection against the possibility of exercise. You can sell calls only by meeting your broker's requirements and obtaining approval to take this high risk. This *margin* requirement applies not only to the writing of options, but also to buying and selling stocks by borrowing from the brokerage firm.

An option writer (seller) hopes that the value of the underlying stock will remain at or below the striking price from the date of sale until expiration. In that case, the option will expire worthless.

As a *writer*, you also have the right to cancel the position at any time by purchasing the option. If time value declines or the underlying stock's value falls, you can cancel the position for a lower purchase price. In that case, you make a profit.

Example: You sell a call and receive a premium of 4. The underlying stock remains below the striking price and time value evaporates. You may buy the option at any time you like and pay a lower price than you received at the point of sale. Or you may allow the option to expire worthless.

Not owning 100 shares is described as a *naked position* and the call itself is called a *naked* or *uncovered option*. The risk of writing an uncovered call is not limited to status at the point of expiration. The buyer has the right to exercise a call *at any time*.

Margin: an account with a brokerage firm that contains a minimum, required amount of cash or securities to provide collateral for short positions, or for purchases made and not paid for until sold

writer: the individual who sells—writes—a call

naked position: the status when the seller does not own 100 shares of the underlying stock, but has sold a call

uncovered option: the same as a naked option, or the opposite of a covered option (when a call is sold and the investor also owns 100 shares)

naked option: an option that is sold to create an open position, when the seller does not own 100 shares of the underlying stock

Example: You sell a call and the underlying stock rises beyond the striking price. However, you have several months before expiration date. The buyer can exercise that call now.

Most calls are not exercised early, but it does happen. You cannot predict whether or not a specific call will be exercised, since buyers and sellers are not matched up one to one. The Options Clearing Corporation (OCC) acts as buyer to every seller and as seller to every buyer. When a buyer exercises, that order is assigned at random to a seller. You won't even know it has happened until your broker informs you that your call has been assigned.

In order to profit from selling calls, the underlying stock must do one of two things.

1. It must remain at or below the striking price, so that it will expire worthless.
2. It must remain at a stable enough price so that the option can later be purchased for a lower premium due to a decline in the time value.

The profit and loss zones for uncovered calls are shown in Figure 5–1. Because you receive cash for selling the option, the break-even point is higher than the striking price. In this example, a call is sold for 5; hence the break-even point (not considering stock or option commissions) is 5 points above the striking price.

Your brokerage firm will require you to put on deposit a percentage of the total potential liability for writing calls. For example, you write one call with a striking price of $40. If the call is exercised, you will have to sell 100 shares at $40 per share. But at that time, the stock could have a market value of $45, 50, or $80 per share.

sell 1 call for 5:

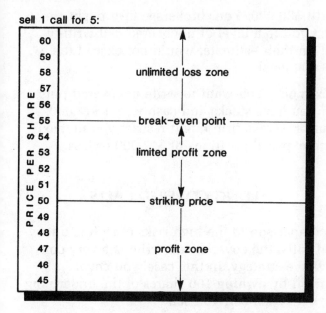

FIGURE 5-1. An Uncovered Call's Profit and Loss Zones

Many of the huge losses investors experienced in October of 1987 resulted from excessive margin activity, some involving calls or puts, or both. Even the brokerage firms did not anticipate the degree of potential loss that resulted. Consequently, many brokerage firms no longer permit the public to write options on margin. If you want to take such a large risk, you will be limited in the amount and degree the brokerage firm will allow. To protect against large losses, you will have to pledge securities already in your account. Different rules may be applied to institutional funders, such as pension plans, mutual funds, and insurance companies.

Example: You want to write uncovered calls in your portfolio. You have stocks and cash worth $20,000. Your brokerage firm might restrict you to a level of uncovered call writing that, in their estimate, would not exceed the $20,000 level.

Example: You want to write uncovered puts, and you have stocks and cash worth $12,000. Your brokerage firm might restrict you to maximum exposed positions of $12,000 or less.

SELLING COVERED CALLS

In comparison to the high risks of selling uncovered calls, the covered call write is a very conservative strategy. In this case, you *cover* yourself by owning 100 shares of the underlying stock for each call you sell.

There are several advantages to the *covered option*.

1. You receive a premium for each option you sell, which is money in your account.
2. Because you are paid for selling the option, the net price of your stock is reduced.
3. A moderate decline in the stock's market value is not a disadvantage as it is if you simply own the stock without writing options.

cover: descriptive of the status when an investor is long in the stock and short in a call option (For each option contract sold, the investor owns 100 shares.)

covered option: a call option that is sold to create an open position, when the investor has 100 shares to cover the short option position

Example: You own 100 shares of stock, which you purchased at $44 per share. You write a September 45 option and are paid a premium of 5. Now your net cost of the stock is $39 per share ($4,400 paid for the 100 shares, less $500 received for the option). If the stock falls in value to between $39 and $44 per share, your investment remains profitable—and you can cancel your option position and realize a profit. The call's premium will be lower than your sales price, and it can be cancelled for less money.

One of three events can take place when you sell a call for every 100 shares you own: an increase in price, a decrease in price, or no significant change. As long as you own 100 shares of stock, any dividends will be paid to you, whether you sell options or not. The value of writing covered calls should be compared to the value of simply buying and holding stock, as shown in Table 5–A.

Before any strategy is undertaken, you should understand the advantages and disadvantages, including the sacrifice of potential profits.

A call seller can *lock in* the price of the un-

lock in: condition of the underlying security when the investor has an offsetting short call (As long as the call is open, the writer is locked in to the striking price, regardless of current market value of the stock; in the event of exercise, the stock must be delivered at that locked in price.)

TABLE 5–A Comparing Strategies

	Outcomes	
	---	---
Event	**Owning Stock and Writing Calls**	**Owning Stock Only**
Stock goes up in value	Call if exercised; profits are limited to striking price and call premium.	Stock can be sold at a profit.
Stock remains at or below the striking price	Time value declines; the call can be closed out at a profit or allowed to expire worthless.	No profit or loss
Stock declines in value	Stock price is discounted by call premium; the call is closed or allowed to expire worthless.	Loss on the stock
Dividends	Earned while stock is held	Earned while stock is held

derlying stock if the call is exercised. Regardless
of how significantly the stock rises, the seller
will receive only the striking price value upon
exercise.

CALCULATING RATE OF RETURN

If your purpose in owning stock is to hold it for
many years, writing calls is not an appropriate
strategy. The call writer's objective is a different
one. It is to produce consistent yields from the
combination of three sources of income:

- Call premium
- Limited capital gains on stock
- Dividends

Example: You own 100 shares you purchased
at $32 per share. The current value is $38, and
you write a March 35 option. You are paid a
premium of 8 ($800), which is an attractive re-
turn. If the call is exercised, you will have
earned $1100 (3 points for the appreciation of
your stock from purchase price to striking price,
plus 8 points for the call premium).

The stock climbs in value to $65 per share,
and your option is exercised. You still earn only
$1100 because you are locked in to the striking
price of $35 per share.

In this example, simply owning the stock
would have been more profitable than selling a
call. In that case, you would have earned $3300.
A covered call writer limits the potential gains
in stock by fixing the striking price. In exchange
for giving up this potential, the call premium

represents immediate income and a limited level of consistent return.

What are the chances of a stock soaring in price? It does happen, but cannot be depended on. If you sell a call and later limit your profits, have you really lost?

You cannot lose profits you never had. One of the pitfalls in covered call writing is to regret the "loss" experienced in those rare cases when a stock does soar.

By accepting the limitation of writing covered calls, you do give up the potential for exceptional gains. But you also *discount* your price, which allows you to have some protection against moderate drops in stock values. You continue to receive dividends. And while you will miss out on the occasional spectacular rise, you settle for consistent and better than average rates of return.

A covered call writer should always identify both the profit and loss zones (shown in Figure 5–2) and also calculate the rate of return.

A covered call's profit and loss zone is determined by the combination of two factors: the option's premium value and the underlying stock's market value. If the stock falls below a break-even point (price paid, less option premium received), that's a loss. Of course, by owning stock, you enjoy the luxury of deciding when to sell; so you can hold stock until the price rebounds. A loss occurs only if you actually sell the stock.

You should never sell a call unless you will be completely satisfied in the event of exercise. For this reason, figuring out your *total* return before you sell a call is so important.

Total return includes stock appreciation, call

discount: a benefit of selling covered calls (The true price of the stock is reduced by the amount of premium received: If the basis in stock is $30 per share and an option is sold for a premium of 5, the basis is discounted to $25 per share.)

total return: the combination of income from the call premium, capital gains in the stock, and any dividends received (Total return should be computed in two ways: if the option is exercised and if it expires worthless.)

covered call profit and loss zones

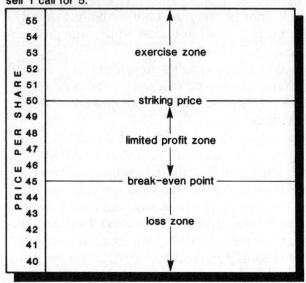

buy stock $50 per share,
sell 1 call for 5:

FIGURE 5–2. A Covered Call's Profit and Loss Zones

premium, and dividends. If the option expires worthless, you enjoy one rate of return; if you close the position by buying the option, your rate of return is different.

Example: You own 100 shares of stock that cost $41 per share. The current value is $44 per share, and you are considering selling a July 45 call. The premium is 5. Between now and expiration, you also expect to receive a total of $40 in dividends.

If the call in this example is exercised, the return will consist of all three elements.

Stock appreciation	$400
Call premium	500
Dividends	40
Total return	$940
Yield (on $4100)	22.9%

If the call is not exercised, but expires worthless, the total return does not include appreciation from the underlying stock. It is still held and will not produce a yield until sold. So return would be

Call premium	$500
Dividends	40
Total return	$540
Yield (on $4100)	13.2%

Although the yield in the second instance is lower, you still own the stock. So you are free to either sell it, or write another call.

TIMING THE DECISION

A first-time call writer might be surprised to experience an immediate exercise. Exercise can occur at any time you are in the money, but you can assume that it will occur at or close to expiration, since that's true in most cases. Nevertheless, the call writer must be prepared to give up 100 shares of stock at any time from the day the call is written until the day of exercise.

As shown in Figure 5–3, during the life of a call, the underlying stock might swing several points above and below the striking price. If you own 100 shares and are considering selling a call, you should keep the following points in mind.

timing and price movement

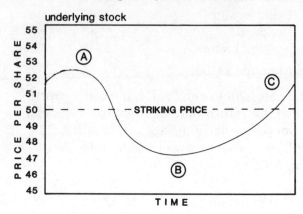

A   in the money – best time
to sell a call

B   out of the money –best
time to buy a call

C   in the money at expiration
– calls will be exercised

FIGURE 5–3. Timing of Call Transactions Relative to Price Movement of Underlying Stock

1. When the striking price of the call is higher than the original cost of the stock, exercise is not negative, since you will profit from both price appreciation and the call premium.
2. If you sell a call for a striking price below the original cost of the stock, you should be sure that the premium is greater than the loss you will have in case of exercise.

Example: You bought 100 shares at $43 per share and sell a call with a striking price of $40. If exercised, you will lose $300 on the stock. So the premium should be greater than 3.

3. In calculating potential yields, you must be sure to allow for commission costs on stock and option, upon purchase, sale, and exercise.
4. For the benefit of a consistent profit from writing calls, you give up the potential for larger gains in the event the stock's price rises.

Selecting an appropriate call depends on the price you originally pay, plus the current price of the stock. An option's premium at various price levels will further affect your decision.

Example: You purchase stock at $51 per share, and it is currently worth $53. Rather than sell the stock, you choose to sell a call with a striking price of $50 and receive a premium of 7 ($700).

The action in this example provides several benefits.

1. If the stock falls in value to below your purchase price, you can buy the option at a profit or allow it to expire worthless.
2. By selling the option, you discount your price from $51 to $44 and gain valuable downside protection if the stock's price declines.
3. You continue to receive dividends.

You might also choose to sell a call that is deep in the money.

Example: You purchased stock at $51 per share, and it is currently worth $53. You will receive at least $500 more by selling a 45 call. But that also increases the chance of exercise. And for the additional premium, you also give up points in the stock's value.

Purchase price	$5100
Exercise value	4500
Loss on the stock	$600

If you receive 11 ($1100) for the call, your net profit will be reduced to only $500 in the event of exercise. You give up $600 by committing to a striking price six points below your original cost.

You should always select options and time your purchases with all of the following points in mind.

- Your original cost
- Amount of the premium
- Relationship of current value to striking price
- Time until expiration
- Total return if the call is exercised and if it expires worthless
- Your objectives in owning the stock and in selling the call (immediate income, downside protection, or long-term growth)

AVOIDING EXERCISE

Assuming that you sell a call on stock you originally purchased because you considered it a worthwhile investment, you might then want to avoid exercise. You must be willing to live with the possibility that your call will be exercised. But many call writers can also benefit by taking action to either defer or completely avoid exercise.

There are several ways to avoid exercise. You cannot depend on an ideal movement in the price of the underlying stock, so you might find yourself in the money and near exercise.

First, to avoid exercise you can cancel an option position by purchasing it, even though you lose on the transaction. In some cases, this action is profitable despite the fact you accept a loss.

Example: You purchased stock at $21 per share and later sold a June 25 call, receiving a premium of 4. The stock is presently valued at $30 per share, and the option premium is at 6. If you buy the option, you will lose $200 on the transaction (original sale at a premium of 4, less closing purchase at 6). However, by avoiding exercise at the striking price of $25 per share, you now own stock with a current market value of $30, which is 3 points higher than your loss.

In selling the call, you had the advantage of downside protection. If the stock had fallen even to $17 per share, you would have been even (original stock at $21, less option premium of 4). But since the stock rose, closing out the option at a loss is a smart move. Considering the current market value of the stock in comparison to the striking price, you are ahead by making this decision. The stock is worth $30, but by closing the call position, you free yourself from the commitment to deliver those shares for $25, which would mean a loss of $600.

Second, you can avoid exercise by exchanging one call for another and at the same time make a profit. Since the premium is higher for options that have a longer period of time to go until ex-

roll forward: the replacement of one call with a call that has the same striking price, but a later expiration date

incremental return: a technique of avoiding exercise when the value of the underlying stock is rising (One call position is closed at a loss, but replaced by two or more new call positions; the net effect of this is to produce a cash profit.)

roll down: the replacement of one call with another that has a lower striking price

roll up: the replacement of one call with a call that has a higher striking price

piration, you gain the advantage of time value if you *roll forward*.

Example: The call you wrote against your 100 shares of stock is near expiration and is in the money. To avoid or delay exercise, you cancel (buy) the original option and sell another one, with the same striking price but a later expiration date.

This technique is possible with single calls, although it is much easier to achieve if you have several hundred shares of stock. The more shares you have, the more the flexibility you have in being able to increase outstanding option contracts as you roll forward adding to your profits. Cancelling a single call and replacing it with two or more options with later expirations, is called *incremental return*. Your profit is increased as you increase the number of outstanding options on your stock.

One type of rolling technique is known as *roll down*.

Example: You originally purchased stock for $31 per share and later sold a call with a striking price of $35. The stock has declined in value, and you cancel (buy) the call position. You then sell another call with a striking price of 30.

A second rolling technique is known as *roll up*.

Example: You orginally purchased stock for $31 per share and later sold a call with a striking price of $35. The stock is now worth $39. You cancel (buy) the first call, accepting a loss, and offset that loss by selling another call with a striking price of 40.

In using the rolling technique, you can exchange an existing call for one that not only has
a later expiration date but also a higher striking
price. See Figure 5–4.

avoiding exercise

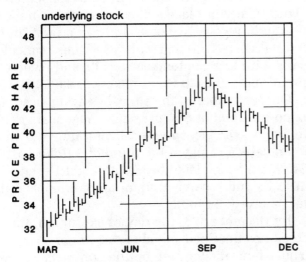

DATE	DESCRIPTION	RECEIVED	PAID
Mar 15	sell 2 Jun 30 calls at 5	$1,000	
Jun 11	buy 2 Jun 30 calls at 8		$1,600
	sell 5 Sep 35 calls at 6	$3,000	
Sep 8	buy 5 Sep 35 calls at 9		$4,500
	sell 8 Dec 40 calls at 6	$4,800	
Dec 22	Dec 40 calls expire worthless	–	–
	totals	$8,800	$6,100
	profit	$2,700	

FIGURE 5–4. Using the Rolling Technique to Avoid
Exercise

Example: You own 800 shares of stock that originally cost $30 per share (total cost, $24,000). You expect the value to rise, but also want to write covered calls. So, on March 15, you sell two June 30 contracts for a premium of 5, and receive $1000.

On June 11, the stock is worth $38 per share, and you know your calls will be exercised. To avoid this, you place a closing purchase transaction to buy your two calls and pay a premium of 8 (total cost, $1600). You replace these canceled calls with five September 35 calls and receive a premium of 6 each (total received, $3000).

On September 8, the stock has again risen and is now valued at $44 per share. You again want to avoid exercise, so you cancel (buy) your five open calls and pay a premium of 9 (total cost, $4500). You replace these with eight December 40 calls and receive a premium of 6 on each (total received, $4800).

By December 22, the day of expiration, the stock has declined in value to $39 per share. Your eight outstanding option contracts expire worthless.

The total profit on this series of transactions is $2700. In addition, you still hold 800 shares of stock now valued at $39 per share, which represents an additional profit of $7,200 should you decide to sell.

This incremental return combining roll up and roll forward techniques demonstrates how exercise can be avoided and profits ensured. Of course, the example is an ideal situation. The stock continued to climb, but finally closed just below the latest striking price. You cannot depend on this pattern to occur with any consistency. But avoiding exercise is a practical and

realistic approach to management of covered
calls when the underlying stock's price is rising.

Stock

Sell 800 shares at $39 per share		$31200
Original cost		24000
Profit on stock		$7200

Options:

Sell 2 June contracts		+1000
Buy 2 June contracts		−1600
Sell 5 September contracts		+3000
Buy 5 September contracts		−4500
Sell 8 December contracts		+4800
Profit on options		3300
Total Profit		$10500

Whenever you roll forward, you benefit from
higher time value: The longer until expiration,
the higher is your income. But you also extend
the period of time you are locked in to the striking price. So for the benefit of extension, you
also lengthen the period of risk.

There is an unlimited number of strategies
you can employ to put off or escape exercise.
The purpose might be simply to avoid having
stock called away, or it might be to increase future income by avoiding an undesirable striking
price level when stock is currently valued much
higher.

Example: You own 200 shares of stock that
you originally purchased at $40 per share. You
have an open June 40 call that you sold for 3.
The stock is now worth $45 per share, and you
would like to avoid being exercised at $40. Ta-
ble 5–B shows the current values of options
available on your stock. A review of this data reveals several rolling opportunities.

TABLE 5–B Current Call Option Values

Striking Price	Expiration Month		
	June	July	Dec.
35	11	13	15
40	6	8	10
45	1	2	5

To begin, you will have to make a closing purchase transaction to buy your June 40 option at 6, accepting a $300 loss on that option. To offset this loss, you can use one of the following strategies.

1. *Strategy 1: Rolling up and Forward.* Sell one December 45 call at 5, producing a net cash increase of $200 ($500 on the December call, less the loss of $300 on the June call).
2. *Strategy 2: Rolling with Incremental Return.* Sell two September 45 calls, and receive $400, producing a net cash increase of $100 ($400 on the September calls, less the loss of $300 on the June call).
3. *Strategy 3: Rolling Forward Only.* Sell one September 40 call at 8, producing a net cash increase of $500 ($800 for the September call, less the loss of $300 on the June call).

If the underlying stock is fairly stable and moves up and down within a range of 5 points, it is possible to sell calls in an indefinite series, thereby cancelling the open positions when time values go out of the premiums. Rolling techniques can then be used when the underlying stock's value moves above or below the typical range.

To show how this strategy works, Table 5–C
gives an actual example of trades over a period
of 2 ½ years. The investor owned 400 shares of
stock and traded with a discount broker. The
sale and purchase prices show the actual cash
transacted, including commissions charged, and
rounded to the nearest dollar. The total net
profit of $2628 occurred after 40 trades (20 buy
orders and 20 sell orders.) Total commission
costs came to $722. So actual gross profits were
$3350, and the investor realized a net of $2628
after the brokerage firm took its share.

The summary in Table 5–C reveals examples
of each type of rolling trade, plus an effective

TABLE 5–C Selling Calls with Rolling Techniques

| Calls Traded | Type | Sold | | Bought | | Profit | Notes |
		Date	Amount	Date	Amount		
1	Jul 35	3/20	$328	4/30	$221	$107	
1	Oct 35	6/27	235	10/8	78	157	
1	Apr 35	1/15	247	4/14	434	−187	
1	Oct 35	4/14	604	6/24	228	376	1
1	Oct 35	7/31	353	9/12	971	−618	
2	Jan 45	9/12	915	12/16	172	743	2
2	Apr 45	12/16	379	2/24	184	195	
4	Jul 40	3/9	1357	5/26	385	972	3
4	Oct 40	6/5	1553	7/22	1036	517	
4	Jan 40	8/5	1504	9/15	1138	366	
		Totals	$7,475		$4,847	$2,628	

1. A roll forward: The loss on the April 35 call was acceptable to avoid exercise, since the
October 35 was profitable.
2. A combination roll forward and roll up: The loss on the October 35 call was acceptable to
avoid exercise at a low striking price. The number of calls was incrementally increased from
one to two.
3. A roll down combined with an incremental return: The number of calls changes from two
to four, and the striking price of 45 was replaced with one for 40.

use of the incremental return technique. The investor was willing to increase the outstanding covered calls on as many as 400 shares of stock in order to avoid exercise when current market value was greater than striking price. And when the stock's price was lower, the investor rolled down, but did not write calls below the original, acceptable striking price of 35.

Any form of covered call writing must be planned ahead of time. Besides the attributes of the option itself, the quality of the underlying stock must be taken into account. If you purchase shares primarily to write calls, chances are you will pick issues that are more volatile than average, as these often have more attractive, higher time values than more conservative stocks.

Whether you intend to write uncovered or covered calls, you will not succeed if you buy over-priced stocks that later fall far below your original cost. An example of an *uncovered call write*, with defined profit and loss zones, is shown in Figure 5–5. In this example, you sell one May 40 call for 2 (+$200). This strategy of selling uncovered options exposes you to unlimited risk. If the stock rises above the striking price beyond the amount of premium received, exercise will create a loss. The stock could rise indefinitely. Upon exercise, you will be expected to deliver 100 shares at the striking price of $40 per share, regardless of current market value.

An example of a *covered call write*, with defined profit and loss zones, is shown in Figure 5–6.

In this example, your own 100 shares of stock that originally cost $38 per share. You now decide to sell one May 40 call for 2 (+$200). This strategy discounts the basis in stock to $36 (pur-

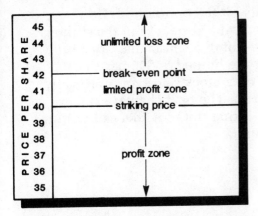

FIGURE 5–5. Example Uncovered Call Write

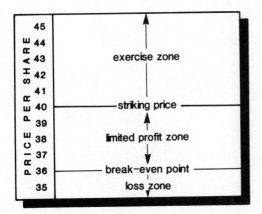

FIGURE 5–6. Example Covered Call Write

chase price of $38, less $200 received for selling the call). As long as the stock's value is at or below the striking price, the call will expire worthless. If it is above that level, the option will be exercised, and your 100 shares will be called away. In that case, your total profit will be $400, consisting of two points in stock appreciation and two points for the option sold. However, selling covered calls also locks in the striking price. In the event of a substantial price increase, profits are limited to $40 per share.

As a call writer, stock selection is critically important to you. The next chapter explains methods for picking stocks with a call-writing strategy in mind.

6

Choosing the Right Stock

You will succeed as a writer of covered calls if you establish a policy for buying the right stocks and then stay with it. The stock you select should suit your ideas of risk and should not be picked based only on current call premium values.

Covered call writing locks in the striking price in the event of exercise. It also locks in an assured minimum profit.

Example: You own 100 shares of stock that cost $38 per share, and you evaluate calls on that stock. A call that expires in three months at the striking price of 40 has a current premium of 4 ($400), and during that period, you will also earn a dividend of $60. Your calculations assure you an annualized profit of 48.4 percent (if the call expires worthless) or of 69.6 percent (if it is exercised).

If the Call Expires

Call premium	$400
Plus dividends	60
Total profit	$460
Basis in stock	$3800

Yield if the option expires
(460 ÷ $3800)   12.1%

Annualized return earned in three months
(12.1% × 4)   48.4%

If the Call Is Exercised

Call premium	$400
Plus dividends	60
Plus capital gain	200
Total profit	$660
Basis in stock	$3800

Yield if the option is exercised
($660 ÷ $3800)   17.4%

Annualized return earned in three months
(17.4% × 4)   69.6%

Note that the annualized return is computed by reflecting yield as if earned in 12 months. So when it takes only three months, the yield percentage is multiplied by four.

DEVELOPING A PRACTICAL APPROACH

Earning a consistently high yield writing calls is not always possible, even for covered call writers. You might be able to sell a call today that is rich in time value, and profit from the combination of capital gains, dividends, and call premium. But the opportunity depends on a combination of factors.

1. The underlying stock is at the right price in relation to your original cost and the call you want to write.
2. The volume of investor interest in the stock and options is high enough to make those calls that rich in time value.
3. The time until expiration is right for your personal goals.

These circumstances might not repeat later. Writing calls requires patience and timing, and you will sometimes have to wait until the yield from writing a call will be just right.

In considering a covered call strategy, a common mistake is to assume that today's circumstances will be there in the future. For example, you might earn 48 percent on your first transaction. But you probably will not be able to *consistently* earn 48 percent. The ideal write will occur in the following circumstances.

1. The striking price is higher than your basis in the underlying stock.
2. The call is in the money, so that it has some intrinsic value.
3. There is enough time until expiration so that the majority of premium consists of time value.
4. Expiration will occur in six months or less, so that you will be locked in for too long.

Example: One investor owns 100 shares of a stock that cost $53 per share. The stock is now valued at $57 per share. One call with a striking price of 55 expires in five months and has a current premium of 6 ($600). All of the ideal circumstances exist: The striking price is 2 points higher than the stock's original cost; the call is in the money by 2 points; two-thirds of the total premium is time value; and expiration will occur in five months. The investor will earn a substantial return whether the call expires worthless or is exercised. And if the high time value disappears from the premium, the short position can be closed at a profit.

This example illustrates a practical and methodical approach to writing covered calls. For the 6 points received from selling the call, the investor also gains 6 points of downside protection. So the net basis in stock is $47 per share (original cost of $53, less 6 points for the call). Even if the stock falls to that level, no money will have been lost.

SELECTING STOCKS FOR CALL WRITING

Some investors choose stocks based only on the potential for yield from covered call writing. This approach is a mistake if other criteria are not applied, because the best-yielding calls often are available on the most volatile stocks. So if you apply the criterion of call writing yield as the sole reason for picking one stock over another, you also increase the chances of wide price swings in your portfolio.

Example: One investor decides to buy stock based on the relationship of current call premium to the price of stock. He has only $4000 to invest, so he reviews only those stocks selling for $40 per share or less. His objective is to buy stock on which the call premium is no less than 10 percent of current value when the call is out of the money or at the money. He prepares a chart:

Current Value	Call Premium
$36	$3
28	3 1/2
25	1
39	4
27	1 3/4

He decides to buy the stock prices at $28 per share, because the call's value is 3½, for a yield of 12.5 percent.

There are several problems with this approach. Most significant is the fact that no distinction is made between stocks. The issue selected is not judged on its own merits, only on the relationship between price and call premium. And by limiting the selection to stocks below $40 per share, the possible market for covered call writing is severely restricted.

There is also a failure to consider the time until expiration. You will receive a higher premium when the expiration date is farther away, but you also lock in the position for a greater period of time.

This approach also fails to judge calls in relation to their current price. Return is increased on the call if it is in the money, which also increases the chance for exercise.

The value of locking in 100 shares to a fixed striking price must always be judged in relationship to the number of months until expiration. For example, a 10 percent or higher yield might be attractive for calls with a three-to-six-month remaining life, but is less attractive when the call does not expire for eight months. Yield is not a constant; it depends on time as well.

Comparing yields between current call premium and stock price also ignores the equally important time factor, potential price appreciation in the stock, and dividend yield.

Covered call writing is a conservative strategy, assuming that you have first selected stocks for their own investment value—not just because covered call writing looks good today.

Benefiting from Price Appreciation

You will profit from covered call writing when the underlying stock's current value is above the price you paid for the stock. In this case, you protect your position against declines in price and also lock in a capital gain in the event of exercise.

Example: You purchased 100 shares of stock last year, when the price was $27 per share. Today, the stock is valued at $38.

In this case, you can afford to write in-the-money calls without risking a loss, or you can write out-of-the-money calls if justified by the amount of time value. Remembering that the original cost was $27 per share, you have four possible courses of action.

1. Write calls with a striking price of 25. You will receive premiums with 13 points of intrinsic value. In the event of exercise, you will lose 2 points (original price, less option striking price), but will keep all of your call premium. And if the stock declines several points, you can cancel (buy) the call and earn a profit.

Example: You sell a call with a striking price of 25. A few weeks later, the stock falls 6 points. You can now cancel the call, and earn a profit of $600, which offsets the price decline.

2. Write calls with a striking price of 30, earning intrinsic value of 8 points. The same strategy applies as in the first example. But this is not as deep in the money, so the chances of early exercise are reduced.

3. Write calls with a striking price of 35. That's only 3 points in the money.

4. Write calls with a striking price of 40 or 45. These are out of the money, so the entire premium is time value. You'll receive less money, but will most likely be able to (a) cancel the position at a profit, or (b) accept a higher exercise and a greater amount of total profit in the future.

If you hold stock that has appreciated in value, you face a dilemma every stockholder must resolve. On the one hand, you are tempted to sell now and take your profits. On the other hand, if the trend is upward, you don't want to sell too soon.

In this situation, covered calls might be the best answer. You provide downside protection with the premium you receive and lock in a capital gain at an attractive price in the event of exercise.

Example: An investor bought stock several years ago at $18 per share. Today, it is worth $35. She sells a call with a striking price of 35 and four months until expiration. The premium, which is 4, is all time value. If the stock falls four points or less, today's price is protected by the call premium. And if the price rises, the investor considers $35 per share an acceptable level of profit.

AVERAGING YOUR COST

average up: a technique for buying stocks when the market value is increasing (By buying shares periodically, the average price is consistently lower than current market value, thereby enabling the covered call writer to sell in-the-money calls when the overall basis in stock is lower than a desirable striking price.)

You can increase your advantage as a call writer if you *average up*, when the price of the stock has risen since your purchase date. You originally bought 100 shares, and the price is now climbing. By buying another 100 shares each time the price increases, your average price will be somewhere in between, as shown in Table 6–A.

How does averaging up help you as a call writer? An investor who buys several hundred shares of stock must be concerned with the risk that prices will fall. So you can start out buying 600 shares today (hoping the price will rise), or you can buy 100 shares per month over a six-month period.

Example 1: An investor buys 600 shares on January 10 at $26 per share. If the price falls to $20, he will have lost $3600 in value. But if the

TABLE 6–A Averaging Up

Date	Shares Purchased	Price per Share	Average Price
January 10	100	$26	$26
February 10	100	28	27
March 10	100	30	28
April 10	100	30	28 1/2
May 10	100	31	29
June 10	100	32	29 1/2

price rises to $32 per share, he will gain $3600 in value.

Example 2: An investor buys 100 shares on the 10th of each month, beginning in January. The price rises each month, and by June 10, her average cost is 29½ per share.

The investor in the second example has reduced risks by buying 100 shares per month. The average price is always less than current market value, but the amount at risk is built up gradually. See Figure 6–1.

The investor who averaged up can sell as many as six calls. Because the average basis is 29½ and current value is 32, the investor can

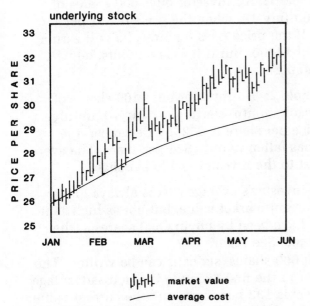

FIGURE 6–1. Example of Averaging Up

average down: a technique for absorbing paper losses on stock investments (By buying shares periodically, the average price is higher than current market value, but part of the paper loss is absorbed on average, thereby enabling covered call writers to profit even when the stock has declined in value.)

sell a call with a striking price of 30 and win in two ways:

- When the average cost is lower than the striking price
- When the call is two points in the money

You also reduce risks and gain advantages as a call writer if you *average down* over time, as shown in Table 6–B.

The risk of buying stock today is that if the price falls, you cannot afford to sell calls. If your basis is higher than the current price, you must sell calls with striking prices below your cost so that, upon exercise, you will lose money on the stock trade. And if you sell higher striking price calls, the premium will be minimal. The solution is averaging down.

Example 1: An investor buys 600 shares of stock on July 10, when the price is $32 per share. If the price rises 8 points, he will earn a profit of $4800. But if it falls 8 points, he will lose $4800.

Example 2: An investor buys 100 shares of stock each month, starting on July 10. In July, the price per share is $32; by December, the price has fallen to only $24 per share. The average cost to the investor is $29 per share.

The investor's average cost is always higher than current market value, but not as high as it would have been by buying 600 shares at the same time. See Figure 6–2.

With 600 shares, six calls can be written. The investor in the first example is at a disadvantage: His basis is $32 per share, and the current value is 8 points lower. He must write calls far out of

TABLE 6–B Averaging Down

Date	Shares Purchased	Price per Share	Average Price
July 10	100	$32	$32
August 10	100	31	31 1/2
September 10	100	30	31
October 10	100	30	30 3/4
November 10	100	27	30
December 10	100	24	29

the money, where premiums will be very small. To lock in 600 shares at a striking price of 30, for example, would not be worthwhile. If exercised, this investor would lose 2 points per share on the stock.

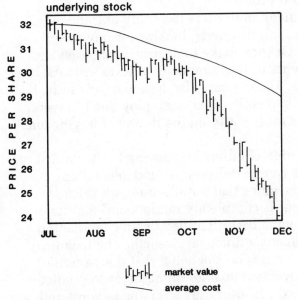

FIGURE 6–2. Example of Averaging Down

The investor in the second example has an average basis of 29. By writing calls with a striking price of 30, this investor will gain 1 point per share if the calls are exercised (before commission costs).

ANALYZING STOCKS

Stocks should be selected not primarily for their potential in covering calls you write, but based on fundamental or technical information, or a combination of the two.

Fundamental analysis is a method of judging the strength and value of stocks based strictly on the financial and economic facts. Fundamentalists study balance sheets, the history of dividend payments, economic prospects of the industry in which the company sells its products or services, and profits.

Technical analysis is the study of trends. Investors follow charts, looking for buy or sell signals. Or they make their decisions based on movements in the composite indexes or stock averages. Technicians also follow trends in insider buy and sell orders or employ one of several methods for identifying the timing of buying and selling stocks.

The value of either fundamental or technical analyses can be debated. A fundamental approach assumes that month-to-month price movement is completely random and that long-term value is best identified by an examination of a company's financial strength. The technical approach relies on the belief that the pattern of price movement enables an observer to predict the immediate future. By studying support and resistance levels, volume trends, and other sta-

fundamental analysis: the study of financial aspects of a company or industry to determine the safety and value of an investment (Fundamentalists believe that future value is determined by historical profits, dividend yield, the P/E ratio, and other financial trends.)

technical analysis: the study of trends and statistics in the market to identify buying and selling opportunities (Technicians believe that price movement is predictable based on historical patterns and trends.)

tistics, market perceptions of value are anticipated, and decisions are based on
interpretations.

Many successful investors, recognizing the
value of both techniques, combine them to identify good values and to time their purchases and
sales.

Call writers must not overlook the importance
of tracking their stocks. There is a tendency to
ignore the changing value of stocks held in a
portfolio, because the call writer is preoccupied
with other concerns: movement of stock price in
relationship to the striking price, chances of exercise, opportunities to roll positions, and other
matters related *just* to the status of the call.

The time will come when, as a call writer,
you will want to close the call position and sell
the stock. For example, you own 100 shares of a
stock on which you have written a number of
covered calls. But now, analysts say that industry's popularity is on the decline. You take this
information as a sell signal and decide to pick a
stock in an industry that has better prospects for
future growth. To make a choice, you can apply
both fundamental and technical tests.

Fundamental Tests

The successful call writer follows not only the
value and status of calls, but also tracks the
stocks on which the calls are written. Several
fundamental guidelines should be followed to
decide when to buy and when to sell.

The current price of a stock reflects the buying
public's *perception* of value. This perception is
affected by changes in the payment and rate of
dividends and by the comparison of the current
price in relation to earnings.

The price/earnings ratio (P/E ratio) is a popular indicator of perceived value. For example, one company earned $220 million in net profits last year and has 35 million shares of stock outstanding. That's $6.29 in earnings per share. The current market value of the stock is $35 per share. The P/E ratio is computed by dividing current market value by the earnings per share:

$$\$35 \div \$6.29 = 5.6$$

Another company earned $95 million and has 40 million shares outstanding, or $2.38 in earnings per share. The stock sells today for $28 per share. The P/E ratio is

$$\$28 \div \$2.38 = 11.8$$

As a general rule, a lower P/E ratio indicates lower risk. So the stock in the first example, with a P/E ratio of 5.6, should be a safer investment than the second one. But the P/E ratio is not always an accurate measurement of total risk. It should be looked at as part of a trend. If, for example, one stock had a P/E ratio last year of 15, and today it's down to 10, that indicates that the price today is more of a bargain than it was a year ago.

The P/E ratio, by itself, is an important fundamental test. But you should also consider several other fundamental factors.

- *Dividend yield:* dividends paid per share, divided by current price
- *Profit margin:* profits divided by sales
- *Profit on invested capital:* net profits divided by the amount of capital outstanding

All of these fundamentals should be reviewed in comparison with past statistics, as part of an overall trend.

The P/E ratio should never be the only indicator you use to decide when to buy or sell. Fundamental analysis should be comprehensive, with a complete study of all the fundamental trends over a period of time.

Technical Tests

Combine fundamental stock tests with technical analysis to develop a well-rounded judgment of the stocks you hold or are considering buying.

One important technical indicator is the trend in volume. You can apply this information against the market as a whole or against a single stock. When volume increases, it indicates increased market interest in that stock. Increased interest can mean that more buyers want shares, but it can also mean that more investors want to sell their holdings. Growth in volume often accompanies significant price movement in either direction.

Chartists (those who track patterns of price movement) look for support levels—prices below which a stock is unlikely to fall—resistance levels—prices above which a stock is unlikely to rise—and breakout patterns—periods when stock prices exceed support or resistance levels. Predicting future price movement depends on tracking average prices over long periods of time and attempting to recognize chart patterns that foretell the direction prices will take.

Another technical indicator for stocks is the high and low price levels. Tracking this information tells you where today's price is in relation

stock evaluation worksheet

stock name _____

DATE	DIVIDEND RATE	P/E RATIO	HIGH	LOW	CLOSE

FIGURE 6–3. Stock Evaluation Worksheet

to the high and low range. For example, most detailed stock listings show the annual high and low. So when a stock has had a range between $26 and $45 per share, and its current value is $44, you know it's at the high end of its range.

Some investors are comfortable buying stocks only when they're in the middle of their range; others look at the overall pattern and buy stocks that show a pattern of growth over time.

No single fundamental or technical test should be used in isolation. The more information you use, the better your chances of timing a smart decision. You can evaluate your stocks as part of a trend, combining both fundamental and technical analysis, by using a stock evaluation worksheet like the one shown in Figure 6–3. After filling in one line for each week or each month, you can look for trends in dividend rate and the P/E ratio (fundamental tests), as well as the high/low and closing price range (technical tests).

APPLYING ANALYSIS TO CALLS

To select stocks on which calls will be written, you need to identify an "acceptable" level of volatility and price change. Volatility is a technical test of a stock's price stability over a period of time. It is usually expressed as a percentage during a twelve-month period and is computed by dividing the annual low by the change in price range.

Example 1: A stock has an annual price range between $21 and $36 per share. Volatility is computed by dividing the difference by the low.

$$\frac{\$36 - \$21}{\$21} = 71.4\%$$

Example 2: A stock has an annual price range between $68 and $63. Its volatility is

$$\frac{\$68 - \$63}{\$63} = 7.9\%$$

The stock in the second example is much less volatile than the one in the first example. For a covered call writer, the smaller swing makes the second stock more predictable, thus more controllable than one with greater volatility.

Fundamental and technical tests can be applied not only to identifying good values in underlying stocks, but also to the timing of selling covered calls.

beta: a measurement of the relative volatility of a stock, made by comparing the degree of price movement to movement in an overall index

A second test worth applying to stocks with covered calls in mind is the *beta*, which is a test of relative volatility—that is, price movement of a stock in relation to the market as a whole. A beta of "1" tells you the stock tends to move to the same degree and in the same direction as the whole market. A beta of "0" implies little or no reaction to market trends, and a beta of "2" is calculated for stocks that react most strongly to market trends or that overreact by moving farther than the market average.

Example: Over the past year, the composite index—the overall value of the market—rose by approximately 7 percent. Your stock also rose by 7 percent, and its beta is 1. If your stock rose 14 percent, its beta would be 2.0.

As a general rule, more volatile stocks will tend to also have higher time value premiums in associated options. That is, time value will also decline at a sharper rate for more volatile stocks than it does for less volatile, more stable ones. The higher time value premium is an indication of the greater risks in buying stock and in writing options on those issues.

Because time value is usually high for a high-beta stock, premium value is also less predictable. It's possible to buy an option and see the expected price movement in the underlying stock—and to still lose money. That's because time value can fall dramatically and in a short period of time.

Example: You buy one call for 5, with a striking price of 45 and three months until expiration, when the underlying stock has a current market value of $41 per share. Over the next two months, the stock rises to $47 per share, or 2 points in the money. But at that point, the call is valued at 4. The time value has declined 3 points, even though the stock rose by 6 points. The proximity of expiration has taken its effect.

Besides volatility and beta of the stock, covered call writers should follow the call's *delta*. The delta is a comparison of changes in an option's premium compared to the movement in the underlying stock. When the option premium and stock price change by the same number of points, the delta is "1." And when the premium changes to a greater or lesser degree, the delta reflects the change in the relationship.

Every change in the price of the underlying stock also affects the value of an option's premium. When an option is deep in the money, the delta approaches 1, so that the premium of that option will change by approximately 1 point in the same direction as price movement of the underlying stock.

When the option is at the money, the delta is

delta: the relationship of change in an option's premium to changes in the price of the underlying stock (When the two move the same number of points, the delta is 1.00; a higher or lower delta can act as a signal to take advantage of adjustments in time value

usually about 0.8. On average, the premium will change by ⁸⁄₁₀ of 1 point for every point of change in the value of the underlying stock.

When the option is out of the money, the delta becomes progressively lower. The farther away from the striking price, the less responsive that option will be to price movement in the stock.

Example: The striking price of a call is 45, and the underlying stock is current valued at $57 per share. Each change in the stock's value will result in a point of change in the call's premium.

Example: An option is at the money. Each change in the value of the underlying stock will affect the option's premium about 80 percent.

Example: A call has a striking price of 65, and the stock's current value is $52 per share. Minor point movements in the stock will have no noticeable effect on the option's premium.

Being aware of the delta enables you to take advantage of conditions and improves the timing, either as a buyer or as a seller.

open interest: the number of open contracts on a particular option (Increases in open interest reflect the *total* contracts outstanding, but does not show whether volume is due to increased activity among buyers or sellers.)

Open interest is another technical indicator that, like the delta, tells you something about the status of a particular option. It is a measurement of the number of option contracts that are currently outstanding. For example, the July 40 calls on a particular stock have an open interest of 30,000 contracts today; last month, only 500 contracts were open. The open interest had increased significantly. Either buyers think the stock will rise in the future, or sellers believe it will fall.

Open interest by itself is of limited value, because you cannot identify whether the activity is created by call buyers or call sellers. But as the

volume of open contracts increases, the trend
tells you that other investors are active.

As expiration nears, you can expect open interest to decline. Open positions are cancelled or
rolled forward as the expiration deadline approaches. Sellers take advantage of a greatly di-
minished time value, and buyers take their
profits. At the point of expiration, open interest
always goes to zero.

Applying the Delta

The delta of a call option should be 1.00 whenever it is well into the money. As a general rule,
the call will increase and decrease one point for
each point of change in the stock's value.

In some cases, the option's delta will change
unexpectedly. For example, an in-the-money call
increases by 3 points when the stock goes up by
only two points (a delta of 1.50). This growth in
time value is a sign that investors perceive that
option to be worth more than its previous price.
See Figure 6–4.

Time value will not move in a predictable pattern, and it will vary from one underlying stock
to another. So as the market perception of future
value (both of the stock and the call) changes,
the time value will also change.

You can track the delta of a call to identify
and time your covered write.

Example: You own 100 shares of a stock you
bought at $58 per share. Yesterday, the stock
rose from $61 to $63, following a rumor that a
tender offer was about to be made. The 60 option's premium rose from from 4 to 8, an increase of 4 points. The delta is 2.00: The stock
rose 2 points, and the option's premium increased by 6.

delta

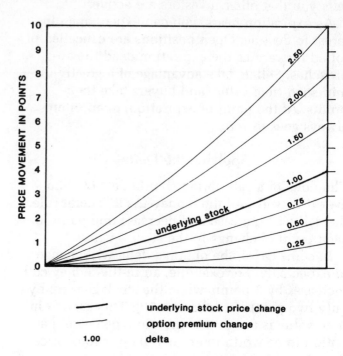

FIGURE 6–4. Changes in an Option's Delta

If a call's premium exceeds the movement in the stock, it can serve as a signal to sell a call. You can use the delta to track market perception, and take advantage of distortions in time value.

The same strategy can be applied when you have an open covered call and are thinking of closing the position. For example, your call is in the money, and the stock falls two points. At the same time, the option's premium falls 3 points, a delta of 1.50. If this is a temporary distortion of time value, you will profit by entering a closing purchase transaction. There is obviously a shift in market perception, and that can serve as a signal that it's time to take action.

FOLLOWING YOUR OWN PERSPECTIVE

All analysis of stocks and calls is estimation. You cannot time your decisions perfectly, but must depend on a combination of fundamental and technical tests to give yourself an edge in the market. As a call writer, do not ignore the importance of studying stocks for more than today's call values. Buy stocks for the same reasons you would as a long-term investor and then use covered call writing as one strategy to increase yields.

Also recognize that covered call writing is a way to provide partial downside protection or to improve overall return on your investment. But writing calls is contrary to your objectives if you want to buy and hold stock for many years.

Example: You bought shares of stock because you believed the company would grow over time. If you sell calls, you risk exercise and might have to give up the stock in the future. The potential for long-term growth is more important to you than current income. In this case, writing calls might not be a smart strategy.

You can certainly avoid exercise by rolling forward or up. But you might run into a situation where price increase is substantial enough so that exercise is unavoidable. Or a call might be exercised early. As a call writer, you must be willing to accept exercise as one possible consequence of your actions. You must be satisfied with the yield you earn in that case, and also with the requirement of actually giving up 100 shares for each call you write.

Do not overlook the importance of tracking stocks and evaluating them on their own merit. By preparing a performance chart like the one shown in Figure 6–5, you can track price movement by the week. A completed chart will help you identify and time a decision to sell or, if you hold onto the stock, the best possible time to write covered calls.

To succeed as a call writer, you must track the option and the stock. Making large percentage profits in calls is of no value if you end up with

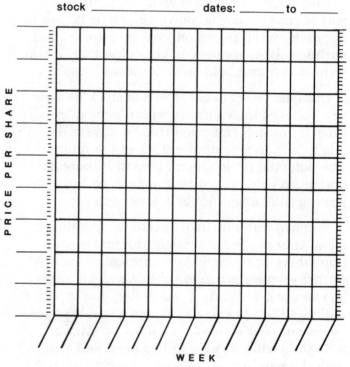

performance chart

stock _____ dates: _____ to _____

FIGURE 6–5. Stock Performance Chart

a portfolio whose current market value is far below your original cost.

Example: An investor bought 100 shares each of four stocks last year and then wrote covered calls. Today, three of the four stocks are several points below the original purchase price. When the total of call profits and dividends are added together, they are less than the paper loss on the portfolio. If the investor sold all shares, it would result in a net loss.

Certainly, this investor's losses would be greater if no calls had been written. The point is that without the covered call writing strategy in mind, would the investor have bought those stocks, or would others have been chosen? Relatively stable, safe stocks tend to have little time value in options, compared to the richer time values in more volatile issues.

Perhaps the greatest risk of call writing is the tendency to buy stocks because calls are attractive bargains. A call writer has the best chance for success if the strategy is secondary. First, pick stocks based on thorough analysis and comparison. Listen to good advice or follow your own instincts, based on your own acceptable level of risk. Be a smart stock investor. Second, time the decision to sell calls on stocks you already own, preferably at a point when current market value is higher than both the striking price of the call and your original cost.

7

Selling Puts

While call sellers must accept the possibility that the underlying stock could rise indefinitely, put sellers take on a more limited risk. A stock's value cannot fall below zero.

A put is an option to sell 100 shares of the underlying stock. So when you sell a put, you grant the buyer the right to sell you those 100 shares. Your risk is that the underlying stock's value will fall. In that case, the put becomes more valuable and will be exercised. But the risk is limited because a decline in price is also limited.

Put sellers can further reduce their risks by choosing puts in a specific striking price range. For example, if you sell puts with striking prices of 50 or more, your maximum loss range is 50 points, or $5000 per 100 shares. But if you sell puts with striking prices of 25 or below, the maximum loss potential is much lower.

EVALUATING STOCK VALUES

If you consider the striking price a fair value for the stock, selling a put achieves two things.

1. You receive immediate cash income from the premium for selling the put.
2. The premium discounts the price of the stock below striking price value.

If you are willing to purchase stock at the striking price, selling a put is a reasonable strategy. But the risk is that prices could fall far below that striking price. If the put is exercised, you will have to purchase shares above the market value at the time of exercise.

Buying shares above market value can be acceptable if you plan to hold stock as a long-term investment. You must be willing to take the paper loss—in the belief that the stock's value will ultimately rise above your price.

Example: An investor sells a put with a striking price of 45 and receives a premium of 6 ($600). She considers $45 per share a good price for the stock. Before expiration, the stock falls to $38 per share, and the put is exercised. The investor is assigned 100 shares and pays $4500, which is 7 points above the current value.

Several points must be made about this example.

1. The outcome is acceptable if the investor still believes that $45 per share is a reasonable price for the stock. If the assumption is correct, the price will eventually rise above that level.
2. The $600 received when the put was sold discounts the real cost of the stock to $39 per

share (45, less 6). So the investor's true basis in the stock is only 1 point per share higher than current market value.

3. The investor would have profited from the sale of the put if the stock's value had risen. The put would not have been exercised and would have expired worthless, and the $600 would have been all profit. So selling puts in a rising market can produce a profit for investors who are unwilling to buy 100 shares.

Put sellers who seek only the income from premiums should select stocks with the best chances for rising in value. So fundamental and technical tests on stocks and the market in general should be applied when selecting underlying securities and their put options. If you do end up purchasing shares upon exercise of a put, you should make certain that you have selected stocks you *want* to own. Receiving income from premiums is only half of the total test. You must also sensibly evaluate the stocks on which those puts are written.

SETTING GOALS

There are four possible goals in selling puts: to produce income, to make use of idle cash deposits in a brokerage account, to eventually buy stocks, or to create a tax put.

Goal 1: Producing Income

The most popular reason for selling puts is to earn income from premiums. Time is on the side of the seller, so selecting puts with a large amount of time value increases the chances for profits.

Example: In January, an investor sells a June 45 put and receives a premium of 4 ($400). At the time, the stock is valued at $46 per share, so that the entire premium represents time value.

If the stock remains at or above $45 per share, the option will eventually expire worthless. If, by exercise date, the stock is valued at between $41 and $45, the investor will make a limited profit. This range is the difference between the striking price and the premium received for the put.

A short position can be cancelled by the writer at any time. But the option can be exercised by the buyer at any time, too. So whenever you sell a put, you must be willing to accept the stock at the striking price. For the income you receive from selling puts, you also accept the risk of having to buy 100 shares of stock below current market value.

A smart put seller is always aware of the potential profit and loss zones and will decide ahead of time when to cancel the position and when to keep it open. See Figure 7–1.

Example: An investor sells a put with a striking price of 50 and receives a premium of 6 ($600). The profit zone is any price at or above the striking price. If the stock falls to between $44 and $50 per share, it is in the limited profit zone ($44 per share is the break-even point because 6 points were received for selling the put). And if the price of the underlying stock falls below $44 per share, it's in the loss zone.

It is conceivable that a put writer could select stocks that will stay at or above the striking

put selling profit and loss zones

sell 1 put for 6:

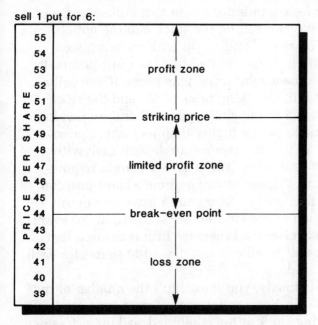

FIGURE 7–1. Put Selling Profit and Loss Zones

price and earn substantial profits over time. But the constant threat of exercise cannot be overlooked.

One of the greatest risks in selling puts is that you will end up with a significantly overpriced portfolio.

Example: An investor sells a number of puts over several months. Four separate puts are exercised, and the investor is assigned 100 shares each of four different stocks. Now his capital is committed to those shares, all of which are higher than current market value. In order to earn a profit from his strategy, the investor must wait until prices rise above his net cost level.

The net cost level is the striking price, less the premium received for the put. You must also allow for commissions paid to a brokerage firm for buying and selling the stock and the option.

The risk of ending up with an overpriced portfolio is not limited to only a few points. It could be a substantial paper loss. If you sell a put with a striking price of 55, and the stock falls to $20 per share, you will end up owning stock 35 points higher than its current price.

You will be required to deposit cash with your brokerage firm to satisfy margin requirements. Whenever you assume a short position, the firm will require you to leave on deposit a portion of the striking price. Then, in the event of exercise, the brokerage firm is assured that you will be able to purchase 100 shares for each put sold.

Obviously, you must limit the number of puts you sell. You cannot exceed your capacity for buying stock at the combined striking prices of open positions.

Example: An investor is willing to invest up to $12,000 in the stock market. She sells puts on several issues, but never exceeds 120 points in striking prices.

This limitation can consist of three options with striking prices of 40 each, of one option with a striking price of 120, or of any combination that does not exceed the maximum level. A broker might allow you to exceed the capacity of your cash balances. But if all your puts are exercised, you will then own stock on margin. Not only must you make up the difference between current value and your own net cost. You must also pay interest on your margin balance.

Whenever you sell puts, you accept the risk of

exercise and cannot cover your position as you can with calls. A call write can be covered (when you own 100 shares) or uncovered. But you cannot cover a written put. A strategy called the covered put write consists of taking a short position in 100 shares of stock for every put sold. But unlike the covered call, your protection extends only the number of points equal to the amount received for the put. If the put's value rises above that level, the short put is not covered. So in practice, a put cannot be fully covered.

Put sellers must view their strategy differently from call sellers. With call writing, exercise is not necessarily a negative, since profits can be built into the strategy. But when a put is exercised, the stock is assigned at a value lower than current market value, without exception.

Put sellers can avoid exercise using the same techniques that call sellers use. Rolling forward provides greater time value and might delay or avoid exercise. However, avoid increasing the number of puts sold on one issue, unless you can afford to buy a greater number of shares and are willing to take that risk. It's a mistake to increase exposure just in an attempt to avoid exercise.

Example: An investor sold a put and received a premium of 3 ($300). The stock declines below the striking price (in the money), and the investor wants to avoid exercise. The original put is now priced at 6 ($600). The investor places a closing purchase transaction and replaces it with two other puts. These have a later expiration date and the same striking price, but are valued at 4 each. He paid $600 to close one position, but received $800 when he opened the new one.

The problem with this technique for avoiding exercise is that risk is doubled. Now, instead of being at risk with one put, the investor has sold two in-the-money puts. If the stock continues to fall, he will be forced to buy 200 shares above current market value.

An alternative is to roll forward with a single put and reduce losses. The investor could have replaced the original position with only one put. Or he could have simply bought the put and accepted the $300 loss. The decision rests with how the stock is viewed at the time it has declined in value. Do you still consider it a bargain at the striking price? If so, exercise should be an acceptable event. If not, you should take the loss and keep your investment capital free for other uses.

You must also compare the potential loss in the put premium to the number of points difference in the stock. For example, the striking price is 45, and the stock has declined to $38 per share, which is 7 points below. If you close your put, you will lose $400.

In this case, a $400 loss is preferable to buying stock that is 7 points above current market value. Once free of the loss, you can sell another put and offset your loss in the first transaction with new premium income.

Goal 2: Using Idle Cash

When investors sell options, the brokerage firm will require either a deposit of cash or securities for at least a portion of the risk. With puts, the maximum risk is easily identified: It's the striking price of the put.

In some cases, investors keep their money on the sidelines, because they believe the stocks they want are overpriced. The dilemma is that if they're wrong and prices go higher, they are not putting their money to work. And if they're right, how long will it take for the market price to correct itself?

One way to deal with these unknown factors is by selling puts on the stocks already selected. You want to keep your money on the sidelines, fearing that prices are too high. By selling puts, you will make a profit if the prices go still higher, and you risk buying stock at the striking price if the stock's price goes lower.

Example: An investor is interested in buying stock, but in her opinion, the market has moved too high too quickly and a correction will occur in the near future. However, the current price of the stock is reasonably low. Her solution is to sell one put for every 100 shares she wants to buy. If the price does rise, the put will lose value and can be cancelled (bought) for a lower price, or it can be allowed to expire worthless. In this way, the investor benefits from a rise in the stock without actually buying shares.

If the stock falls, the investor will be assigned 100 shares for each put sold. As long as the striking price is fair in the investor's opinion, a decline in price is not of great concern. Because the investor intends to hold those shares for the long term, the difference between purchase price and current value is only a temporary problem.

Because the money is already in the brokerage account, the broker knows that the investor can afford to buy 100 shares, because money is there equal to or greater than the striking price.

Goal 3: Buying Stock

Another reason for selling puts is to intention-
ally seek exercise. Selling the put discounts the
price by the amount of premium, and the investor is not concerned with price drops between
now and the expiration date.

Example: You want to buy 100 shares of stock
at $40 per share. The current price is $45, and
you can sell a November 45 option for a premium of 6 ($600). That will reduce your net
price to $39 per share.

In this case, the put is at the money, and the
premium—all time value—is attractive. Even if
the price falls far enough so that current value is
below $40 per share, your long-term plans are
not changed. If, though, the price of stock rises
and the put expires worthless, you keep the
$600 premium and can now adjust your goal.
You can purchase stock at $46 per share or
lower, now that you've earned a $500 profit from
selling the put. On a net basis, the stock will
still cost you only $40 per share.

This process could be repeated indefinitely, as
long as the put you sell expires worthless and
the stock remains out of the money. Eventually,
you will achieve exercise and buy the 100 shares
of stock at what you consider an acceptable
price.

Applying this idea, you do risk losing a buying opportunity. If the stock rises too far too
quickly, you cannot make up the difference in
premium income.

Example: You want to buy stock at $40 per
share, and it is currently valued at $45. So you
sell a put with a striking price of 45 and receive

a premium of 6. But the stock rises 14 points by expiration.

Your put expires worthless and the $600 you received is profit. But if you had bought 100 shares instead of selling a put, you would have earned $1400 in profit.

To succeed as a put seller, you must be willing to risk losing money in two ways: due to unexpected price movement in the stock.

1. If the price of the underlying stock rises beyond the amount you receive in premium, you miss the opportunity to make a profitable investment. You settle for the premium only. This situation is not entirely negative. You still have your capital as security for future put sales and could make up the loss by following a continuing selling strategy.

2. If the price of the underlying stock falls drastically, you will be forced to purchase 100 shares at a price far above current market value. It may take a lot of time to make up the difference. And your capital is tied up in that stock, preventing you from pursuing put writing strategies at the level you want.

While the risks of put selling are more limited than they are for call selling, you could lose profit opportunities in the event the stock moves more points than the premium you receive—in either direction.

Goal 4: Creating a Tax Put

A fourth reason to sell puts is to create an advantage for tax purposes, known as a *tax put.* However, before employing this strategy, you

tax put: a strategy involving the sale of stock at a loss—taken for tax purposes—and the sale of a put. (The premium on the put eliminates the loss on sale of stock: If exercised, the investor buys back the stock at the striking price.)

should first check with a professional tax adviser.

An investor who has a paper loss on stock (where current market value is lower than the original purchase price) sells that stock to create a realized loss. This loss is deducted on that year's tax return. At the same time, the investor sells a put on the same stock, and the premium received offsets the amount of the loss.

One of three results is possible.

1. The stock's market value rises, and the option is allowed to expire worthless. In this case, the investor has escaped the loss situation, taken a tax write-off on the stock, and reports a gain on the option premium in the following year.

2. The stock's value rises and the investor closes the position, buying the put at a lower price than it was sold for.

3. The stock falls below the striking price, and the investor is assigned the stock. In this case, the overall basis in the stock should be lower than the original cost.

It must be assumed that if the stock is currently lower than its original cost, then the put will have a striking price that is also below that cost. So upon exercise, the investor not only keeps the premium; the basis in the stock is also lowered.

The advantage to a tax put is twofold. First, you take a tax loss on the stock in the year it is sold, deferring the gain on the option premium until the following year. And second, you profit from selling the put option, as shown in Figure 7–2, in the following ways.

1. The premium income received offsets the loss.
2. In the event of exercise, the true basis in the stock is reduced from the original cost to the striking price.

Example: You originally bought stock at $38 per share, and it is now valued at $34. You sell the stock and realize a $400 loss. At the same time, you sell a put with a striking price of 35 and receive a premium of 6. If exercised, the result of this strategy is, first, that your $400 loss in stock is more than offset by the $600 income

tax put

DATE	ACTION	RECEIVED	PAID
Aug. 15	buy 100 shares at $50		$5,000
Dec. 15	sell 100 shares at $47	$4,700	
Dec. 15	sell 1 Feb 50 put at 6	600	
	total	$5,300	$5,000
	net cash	$ 300	

PRICE MOVEMENT	RESULT
stock rises above striking price	$300 profit
	put is bought at a profit
stock falls below striking price	put is exercised at $50, net cost $47 (with $300 profit from tax put)

FIGURE 7–2. Example Tax Put

in put premium. Your net adjusted basis is now
$36 (original purchase of $38 per share, less the
$200 net profit from the tax put). Second, when
the put is exercised, you buy 100 shares of stock
at the striking price of 35, which is only one
point below your adjusted basis.

Put sellers enjoy an important advantage over
call sellers. The risk is not unlimited by the potential for indefinite price increases. A stock can
only fall so far that it becomes worthless.

An example of a put write, with defined profit
and loss zones, is shown in Figure 7–3. In this
example, you sell one May 40 put for 3 (+ $300).
The outcome of this short position in puts will
be profitable if the stock remains at or above the
striking price. If, at expiration, the value is lower
than $40 per share, you will have 100 shares put
to you and will purchase them at the striking
price. Put selling involves a limited form of risk.
With uncovered calls, the price of stock could
rise indefinitely. But it can fall only to zero. Because you receive $300 for selling the put, the
break-even price is 3 points below the striking
price.

The greatest risk a put seller undertakes is
that stock will become worthless. In that event,
the entire striking price value will be lost. This
risk is virtually eliminated by selecting stocks of
companies with a solid fundamental strength
and reasonable long-term prospects.

As with all option strategies, the best stocks
for a put writing strategy are those that tend to
move in a limited price range, thereby offering
enough volatility to create short-term profits, but
not enough so that there is great risk.

Put sellers must be willing to actually accept
100 shares that will be valued below current

put write

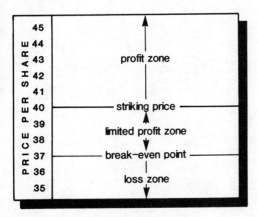

FIGURE 7–3. Example Put Write

market value in the event of exercise. If the current price is reasonable in your point of view, and if you have thoroughly studied the company's strength and prospects for future growth, selling puts can be a smart way to increase income, discount the price of stocks you end up buying, and benefit from price increases without having to buy stock now.

In the next chapter, you will see how buying and selling strategies can be combined to increase income and reduce—or increase—risks.

8

Combined Techniques

There are only four basic strategies in option investing: buying or selling with either puts or calls. But these four approaches can be combined in a variety of ways: long and short positions opened together, covered and uncovered options that offset one another, and mixtures that result in profits if the underlying stock moves in either direction.

Many of these strategies involve taking short positions in options. Remember that selling calls and puts involves considerable risk. If you cover a call position, that risk is reduced. And to an extent, short put positions can be protected.

In this chapter, spreads, straddles, and hedges will be explained. A *spread* involves opening both long and short positions in options on the same underlying stock, but with different striking prices or expiration dates. Whenever the striking prices are identical in a spread strategy, it is called a *vertical spread*, or a *money spread*.

spread: the simultaneous purchase and sale of options —on the same underlying stock— with different striking prices or expiration dates or both. (The purpose is to increase the potential for profits, while reducing risks if the underlying stock's movement exceeds what is anticipated, or to take advantage of the timing of stock price movement.)

vertical spread: any bull or bear spread that involves options with different striking prices, but identical expiration dates

money spread: another term for the vertical spread

combination: any multiple purchase and/or sale of related securities whose terms are not identical

straddle: the simultaneous purchase and sale of the same number of calls and puts with identical striking prices and expiration dates

hedge: a strategy in which one position protects the other (Buying a put is a form of hedge to protect the value of 100 shares of the underlying stock.)

You can also create spread positions by buying and selling options that vary by expiration date or that are a *combination* of the differences in striking price and expiration.

A *straddle* is the purchase and sale of equal numbers of calls and puts with identical terms. And a *hedge* is the opening of two or more different security positions, for the purpose of reducing risk.

Most investors new to the options market will want to keep their strategies fairly simple at first. If you do venture beyond simple strategies, you are most likely to employ the vertical spread. Other, more advanced strategies are complex and beyond the scope and intention of this book. They are included here only to explain the entire range of possibilities in option trading. Considering the risks, commission costs, and complex analysis involved in advanced option strategies, they should be avoided by all but the most experienced investors.

Remember that what looks safe on paper might not always work out profitably. If you plan to use any of the advanced strategies— spreads, hedges, or straddles—you should first ensure that you fully understand all of the risks and costs of those moves, and that you have the knowledge and experience to proceed.

UNDERSTANDING VERTICAL SPREADS

Option investors use the spread to take advantage of the predictable course of changes in premium value. You can generally assume that when an option is in the money, its price will change more rapidly than when it is out of the money.

With this assumption in mind, you have an advantage when you open offsetting long and short positions. The position that is in the money will increase or decrease in price at a faster rate than the offsetting option.

Bull and Bear Spreads

There are two broad types of spreads: bull and bear. A bull spread provides the greatest profit potential if the underlying stock's value increases. And a bear spread will be most profitable if the stock's value falls.

In a bull spread, an option with a lower striking price is bought, and one with a higher striking price is sold. In a bear spread, the opposite is true. So there are four possible forms of spread: bull spreads using either calls or puts and bear spreads using either calls or puts.

Example: As shown in the example in Figure 8–1, you open a bull spread using calls. You sell one December 55 call and buy one December 50 call. At the time, the underlying stock is valued at $49 per share. When the stock has risen to $54 per share, the December 50 call will have increased in value point for point with the stock because it is in the money. The short position call, at 55, will not change in value to the same degree. At this point, the position can be closed at a profit.

A *bull vertical spread* will be profitable when the price of the underlying stock moves in the direction anticipated. That is, a bull spread involves buying the lower-priced option in the hope that the stock will increase in value between now and expiration. In that case, the long in-the-money option will increase in value at a faster rate than the higher, short option.

bull vertical spread: the purchase and sale of calls or puts that will create maximum profits when the value of the underlying security rises (Options with a lower striking price are bought, and an equal number of options with a higher striking price are sold.)

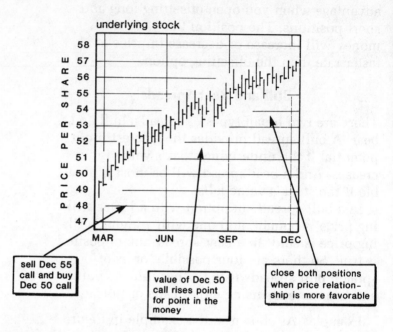

FIGURE 8–1. Example Bull Spread

A detailed bull vertical spread, with defined profit and loss zones, is shown in Figure 8–2. In this example you sell one September 45 call for 2 (+$200) and buy 1 Sep 40 call for 5 (−$500) at a net cost of $300. When the stock rises between $40 and $45 per share, the value of the September 40 call will increase dollar for dollar with the stock, while the short September 45 call will not rise in value as quickly. Up to the $45 per share level, the spread can be closed at a profit (assuming the difference in option values exceeds the cost of $300). Above the $45 per share level, the spread of 5 points in striking prices is offset by the long and short positions.

bull vertical spread

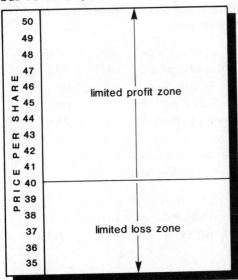

FIGURE 8–2. Bull Vertical Spread Profit and Loss Zones

Thus, maximum profits are limited and so are maximum losses.

A bull spread can also be entered using puts, in which case the in-the-money higher put will *lose* value more rapidly than the lower, long put.

Example: You open a bull spread using puts. You sell one October 55 put and buy one October 50 put. At the time, the underlying stock is valued at $52 per share. Because the higher strike is in the money, the premium value is greater than the lower, out-of-the-money put. So as the stock's price rises, the short put will lose its premium faster than the long put. The position can then be closed at a profit.

A *bear vertical spread* will be most profitable when the stock's value falls. In this spread, the

bear vertical spread: the purchase and sale of calls or puts that will create maximum profits when the value of the underlying security falls (Options with a higher striking price are bought, and an equal number of options with a lower striking price are sold.)

higher valued option is always bought, and the lower valued one is sold. The spread can be entered using calls or puts.

Example 1: You open a bear spread using calls. You sell one October 50 call and buy one October 55 call. At the time, the underlying stock's value is at $47 per share. The premium value of the lower in-the-money call will decline point for point with the underlying stock. As the gap between the two premium values narrows, you can close the position at a profit.

Example 2: You open a bear spread using puts. As shown in the example in Figure 8–3, you sell one December 50 put and buy one De-

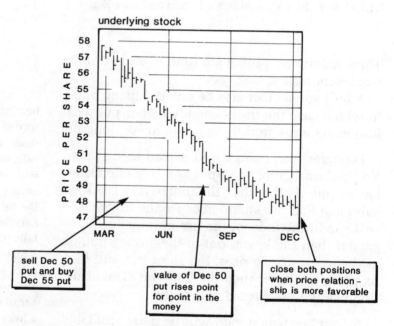

bear spread

FIGURE 8–3. Example Bear Spread

cember 55 put. The underlying stock's current
value is $55 per share. As the price moves
down, the value of your long put will increase
point for point with the stock, while the short
put will gain less. By the time the stock's value
has declined to $51 per share, the position can
be closed at a profit.

A detailed bear vertical spread, with defined
profit and loss zones, is shown in Figure 8–4. In
this example; you sell one September 40 call for
5 (+$500) and buy one September 45 call for 2
(−$200), with net proceeds of $300. As the
stock's value falls below $45 per share, the short
call (at 40) will lose value point for point; the
lower long call will not react to the same degree.
As the $40 per share level is approached, the

bear vertical spread

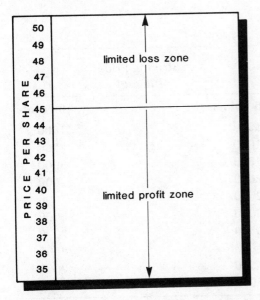

FIGURE 8–4. Bear Vertical Spread Profit and Loss Zones

spread can be closed for a profit. (Had this example employed puts, the higher in-the-money long put would have increased in value point for point with a decline in the stock's value.)

In this call example, the profit will be frozen once both calls are in the money—that is, when the underlying stock falls below $40 per share. At that point, the long and short positions offset, and the level of profit will be frozen.

In all of these examples, the risk is that the stock will move against the spread. You should close the spread before the short position gains value. However, if the underlying stock's value changes too quickly, you risk exercise or might have to close at a loss or reduced profit. In that event, your maximum risk is limited to the difference in the two striking prices, multiplied by the number of options involved. See Table 8–A

TABLE 8–A Spread Risk Table

Number of Options in Spread	Striking Price Interval	
	5 Points	**10 Points**
1	$500	$1000
2	1000	2000
3	1500	3000
4	2000	4000
5	2500	5000
6	3000	6000
7	3500	7000
8	4000	8000
9	4500	9000
10	5000	10,000

Example: You open a spread involving the purchase of one option and the sale of one option. The difference in striking prices is 5 points. Your maximum risk is $500.

Example: You open a spread involving the purchase of four options and the sale of four options. The difference in striking prices is 10 points. Your maximum risk is $4000 (striking price difference of 10 points, multiplied by the number of options).

Box Spreads

You can open a bull spread and a bear spread at the same time by using options on the same underlying stock. In this case, your risk is still limited, whether the stock rises or falls in value. This strategy is called a *box spread*.

A box spread is the simultaneous opening of a bull spread and a bear spread, on the same underlying security. A limited profit can be earned if the stock moves in either direction.

box spread: the opening of a bull spread and a bear spread at the same time and on the same underlying stock (The investor will maximize profits when the stock rises or falls in value.)

Example: As illustrated in Figure 8–5, you create a box spread by buying and selling the following positions.

1. *Bull spread:* Sell one September 40 put and buy one September 35 put.
2. *Bear Spread:* Buy one September 45 call and sell one September 40 call.

If the price of the underlying stock moves significantly in either direction, portions of the box spread can be closed. Of course, this action will create an uncovered option. But if the stock's price then reverses, you can profit from price movements in both directions.

box spread

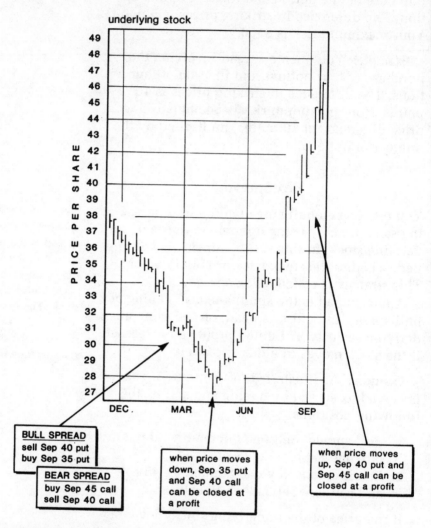

underlying stock

BULL SPREAD
sell Sep 40 put
buy Sep 35 put

BEAR SPREAD
buy Sep 45 call
sell Sep 40 call

when price moves
down, Sep 35 put
and Sep 40 call
can be closed at
a profit

when price moves
up, Sep 40 put and
Sep 45 call can be
closed at a profit

FIGURE 8–5. Example Box Spread

box spread

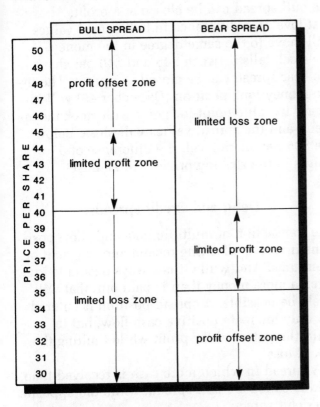

FIGURE 8–6. Box Spread Profit and Loss Zones

A detailed box spread, with defined profit and loss zones, is shown in Figure 8–6. The net proceeds from this box spread result from the following transactions.

1. *Bull*: Sell one September 45 put for 6 (+$600) and buy one September 40 put for 2 (−$200).
2. *Bear*: Sell one December 35 put for 1 (+$100) and buy one December 40 put for 4 (−$400).

credit spread: any spread in which the receipts from short positions exceed the cost of long positions (For example, a May 40 call is sold for a premium of 6 and a May 45 call is bought for a premium of 1, with a net credit of 5 ($500) before commissions.)

debit spread: any spread in which the receipts from short positions are less than the cost of long positions (For example, a June 55 call is sold for a premium of 2 and a June 50 call is bought for a premium of 6, with a net debit of 4 ($400).)

If the stock rises between $40 and $45 per share, the bull spread can be closed at a profit. Above that level, the difference in bull spread values will move to the same degree in the money. If the stock falls between $45 and $40 per share, the bear spread can be closed at a profit. The in-the-money long position (December 40) will increase in value point for point with stock movement, and the spread values will close. Below the $35 per share level, the difference of 5 points in the striking prices will be offset.

Debit and Credit Spreads

The transaction of multiple long and short positions involves offsetting receipt and payment of premiums. And while it is always desirable to receive more money than is paid out, that will rarely be possible. A spread position is entered not only to create positive cash flow, but to build the potential for profit while limiting the risk of loss.

A spread in which more cash is received than paid is called a *credit spread*, while the opposite is a *debit spread*.

UNDERSTANDING DIAGONAL AND HORIZONTAL SPREADS

In the previous section, examples were given of vertical spreads—that is, options entered with identical expiration dates but different striking prices. Beyond the vertical spread is a more complex form, which varies by time of expiration. Called *calendar spreads* or *time spreads*, these come in two broad types.

1. *Horizontal spread*: You use options that have the same striking price but different expiration dates.
2. *Diagonal spread*: You use options that have different striking prices *and* expiration dates.

Example: You sell one March 40 call for 2 (+$200) and buy one June 40 calls for 5 (−$500) at a net cost of $300. This horizontal calendar spread involves two expiration periods. The earlier call is short, and the later one is long. In the event of exercise, the risk is limited to $300, which is the net amount spent on options. If the March call is exercised, it can be offset by the June call. Thus, the loss is limited both in amount and time. (See Figure 8–7.) If, by the March expiration, there is no exercise, the first call expires worthless, and the second phase

calendar spread: a strategy in which options bought and sold on the same underlying stock have different expiration dates

time spread: another term for a calendar spread

horizontal spread: a calendar spread in which the offsetting options have the same striking price but different expiration dates

diagonal spread: a calendar spread in which the offsetting options have both different striking prices and different expiration dates

horizontal calendar spread

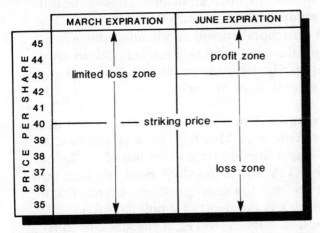

FIGURE 8–7. Profit and Loss Zones for Example Horizontal Calendar Spread

of the strategy goes into effect. Now, with the short position eliminated, only the long position remains. If the stock rises more than 3 points above the striking price, it can be sold at a profit.

Example: You sell one March 40 call for 2 ($+\$200$) and buy one June 45 call for 3 ($-\$300$) at a net cost of $100. This diagonal calendar spread involves both different expiration months and striking prices. If the earlier short call is exercised, the later long call can be used to offset. Until the earlier expiration, the risk is limited to the net cost of the two calls. After that, the break-even point is the higher striking price, plus the net cost of options ($45, plus 1 point), or $46 per share. (See Figure 8–8.) If the underlying stock increases in value above that point, the June 45 call can be sold at a profit.

Giving spread strategies directional names of vertical, horizontal, and diagonal helps visualize the different spread strategies. These concepts are summarized in Figure 8–9.

A horizontal spread is advantageous when time values between two related options are temporarily distorted or when a later option protects the risks of an earlier one.

Example: You open a horizontal spread using calls. You sell a March 40 for a premium of 4 and buy a June 40 for a premium of 6. The net cost is 2 ($200). If the stock rises, the long position protects the short position, so your maximum risk is the debit of 2 points in the offsetting calls. However, if the stock remains at or below the striking price between now and expiration, it will expire worthless. At that point,

diagonal calendar spread

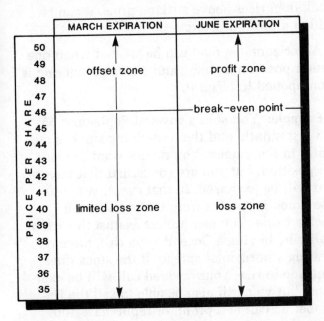

FIGURE 8–8. Profit and Loss Zones for Example Diagonal Calendar Spread

spread strategies

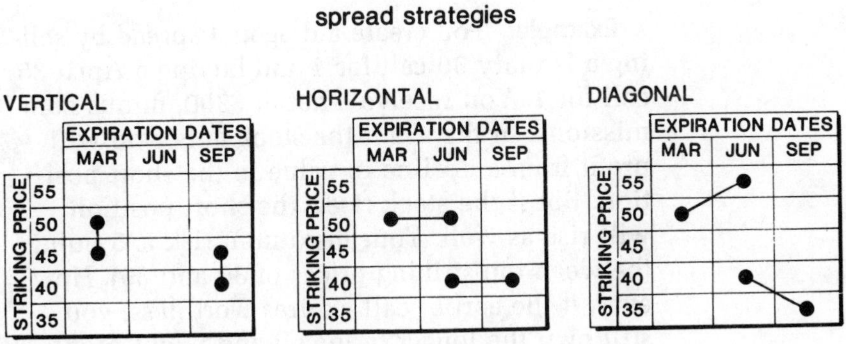

FIGURE 8–9. Comparison of Spread Strategies

you will still own the long June 40 call. If the stock then rises above striking price, it can be sold at a profit or exercised.

A horizontal spread can be created when one option position is open, and a subsequent one is then opened to offset it.

Example: You sold a covered September 55 call last month, and the underlying stock is currently in the money. You do not want to close the position, but you are concerned that the option will be exercised. In that event, you will lose potential profits from increases in the stock's value. You can protect against this eventuality by buying a December 55 call, thereby creating a horizontal spread. If the stock does continue to rise, your covered call will be exercised, but you will also be able to sell the December 55 call at a profit, or repurchase 100 shares by exercise.

A diagonal spread is a combination of vertical and horizontal features. Long and short positions are opened with different striking prices and expiration dates.

Example: You create a diagonal spread by selling a January 30 call for 4 and buying a April 35 call for 1. You receive a net of $300, minus commissions. In the event the stock falls, you will profit from a decline in value in the short position. But if the stock rises, the short position will rise as well. Your maximum risk is 5 points (between the striking prices of 30 and 35). However, if the earlier call expires worthless, you still own the longer term call and might profit from later price appreciation.

ALTERING SPREAD PATTERNS

The vertical, horizontal, and diagonal patterns of the typical spread can be employed to reduce risk. Going beyond this, spread techniques can be expanded through the ratio or butterfly strategies.

Ratio Calendar Spread

The ratio calendar spread involves not only employing different numbers of options on either the long or short side but also varying the strategy by expiration month.

Example: You enter into a ratio calendar spread by selling four May 50 calls at 5 and buying two August 50 calls at 6. You receive a net of $800 before commissions. Between now and the May expiration, you depend on the underlying stock remaining at or below the striking price in order to profit. The break-even point is $54 per share.

If the stock is at $54 per share at the point of expiration, you will break even due to the ratio of 4 short calls to 2 long calls. Upon exercise, the two uncovered calls will cost $800, which is the same amount as the credit received when the position was opened. If the price of the stock is higher than $54 per shares, the loss occurs at a 4 to 2 ratio. If the May expiration date passes without expiration, the four short positions are profitable, and you still own two August 50 calls.

The profit and loss zones in this example are shown in Figure 8–10. Note that no consideration is given to the following factors:

ratio calendar spread: a strategy in which the number of options bought is different from the number sold and in which the expiration dates of the options on each side differ (This strategy establishes two profit/loss zones, one of which disappears upon the earlier expiration.)

- Cost of commissions
- Time value of longer term premiums
- Outcome in the event of an unexpected early exercise

A complete *ratio calendar spread* strategy, with defined profit and loss zones, is illustrated in Figure 8–11. In this example, you sell five June 40 calls for 5 (+ $2500) and buy three September 40 calls for 7 (− $2100), with net pro-

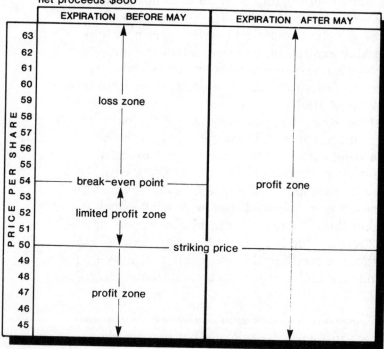

sell 4 May 50 calls for 5,
buy 2 Aug 50 calls for 6:
net proceeds $800

FIGURE 8–10. Example Ratio Calendar Spread

ratio calendar spread

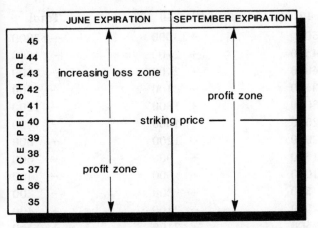

FIGURE 8–11. Ratio Calendar Spread Profit and Loss Zones

ceeds of $400. This ratio calendar spread strategy involves long and short positions and two expiration months. The short position risk is limited to the first expiration period, with losses partially hedged by the later long positions. As long as the stock does not rise above the striking price of the June 40 calls, the short side of the spread will expire worthless. However, you have two uncovered options up until that point (net of five short and two long calls).

Once the June expiration has passed, the $400 net received is profit, regardless of stock price movement. However, if the stock rises above the striking price, you will earn 3 points for every point of increase in-the-money (with three long calls still open).

Table 8–B provides a summary of values for this strategy at various stock prices as of expiration. If the stock remains at or below the $40 per share level, the proceeds of the ratio calendar

TABLE 8–B Profits/Losses for Ratio Calendar Spread Example

Price	Jun 40	Sep 40	Total
$50	− $5000	+ $3000	− $2000
49	− 4500	+ 2700	− 1800
48	− 4000	+ 2400	− 1600
47	− 3500	+ 2100	− 1400
46	− 3000	+ 1800	− 1200
45	− 2500	+ 1500	− 1000
44	− 2000	+ 1200	− 800
43	− 1500	+ 900	− 600
42	− 1000	+ 600	− 400
41	− 500	+ 300	− 200
40	+ 2500	− 2100	+ 400
39	+ 2500	− 2100	+ 400
38	+ 2500	− 2100	+ 400
lower	+ 2500	− 2100	+ 400

spread are profit. However, the profit will never exceed this level. The loss, though, increases in the event of price increase in the underlying stock—by 2 points for every point of change.

Ratio Calendar Combination Spread

The ratio calendar spread strategy can be expanded into a ratio calendar combination, which adds the ratio approach to a box spread.

Example: As illustrated in Figure 8–12, you transact the following options.

- Buy one June 30 call at 3 (− $300).
- Sell two March 30 calls at 1 ¾ (+ $350).
- Buy one September 25 put at ¾ (− $75).
- Sell two June 25 puts at ⅝ (+ $125).

ratio calendar combination

buy 1 Jun 30 call for 3 (−300)
sell 2 Mar 30 calls for 1¾ (+350)
buy 1 Sep 25 put for ¾ (− 75)
sell 2 Jun 25 puts for ⅝ (+125)
net proceeds $100

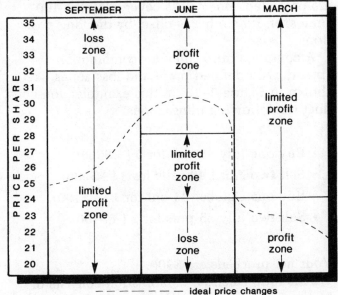

FIGURE 8–12. Example Ratio Calendar Combination

The total adds to net proceeds of $100, without figuring commissions. This complex combination involves 2 to 1 ratios between short and long positions on both sides (two short options for each long option). In the event of unfavorable price movements in either direction, you risk exercise. The ideal price change will enable you to close segments of the combination before expiration dates.

Considering commission costs, entering combinations with one or two options on either side

ratio calendar combination spread: a strategy involving both a ratio between purchases and sales and a box spread (Long and short positions are opened in the same security but in varying numbers of contracts and with expiration dates extending over two or more periods in order to produce profits during periods of price increases or decreases in the underlying stock.)

is a costly strategy—especially considering the slim profit potential and wider risk of loss. That risk is somewhat reduced if shares of the underlying stock are owned. For example, when writing two calls and selling one, the risk of a price increase is eliminated because all call positions are protected. One call is covered by the 100 shares, and the other is offset by the long position.

A complete *ratio calendar combination spread*, with defined profit and loss zones, is shown in Figure 8–13. In this example; you conduct the following transactions.

- Buy one July 40 call for 6 (−$600).
- Sell two April 40 calls for 3 (+$600).
- Buy one October 35 put for 1 (−$100).
- Sell two July 35 puts for 2 (+$400).

Your net proceeds are $300.

This ratio calendar combination consists of two separate ratio calendar spreads. Profits can occur if the stock moves in either direction, and maximum losses are limited. There are three separate expiration dates involved. One danger of this strategy is that, as earlier options expire, the later option positions become more exposed to loss, and risk can increase. This situation can be reversed—so that the chance for later profits is made greater—if a combination is built using later long positions instead of short ones. Table 8–C gives a breakdown of the profits or losses that will be produced at various prices as of expiration for the ratio calendar combination spread example in Figure 8–11.

ratio calendar combination

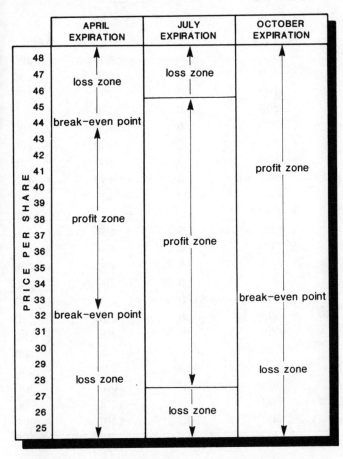

FIGURE 8–13. Ratio Calendar Combination Profit and Loss Zones

Butterfly Spreads

Another spreading technique is the butterfly pattern. This strategy involves offsetting options in a middle striking price range with opposite positions above and below.

TABLE 8–C Profits/Losses for Ratio Calendar Combination Spread Example

Price	Apr 40 Call	Jul 40 Call	Jul 35 Put	Oct 35 Put	Total
$47	+$100	−$800	0	+$400	−$300
46	0	− 600	0	+ 400	− 200
45	− 100	− 400	0	+ 400	− 100
44	− 200	− 200	0	+ 400	0
43	− 300	0	0	+ 400	+ 100
42	− 400	+ 200	0	+ 400	+ 200
41	− 500	+ 400	0	+ 400	+ 300
40	− 600	+ 600	0	+ 400	+ 400
39	− 600	+ 600	0	+ 400	+ 400
38	− 600	+ 600	0	+ 400	+ 400
37	− 600	+ 600	0	+ 400	+ 400
36	− 600	+ 600	0	+ 400	+ 400
35	− 600	+ 600	0	+ 400	+ 400
34	− 600	+ 600	0	+ 200	+ 200
33	− 600	+ 600	+$100	0	+ 100
32	− 600	+ 600	+ 200	− 200	0
31	− 600	+ 600	+ 300	− 400	− 100
30	− 600	+ 600	+ 400	− 600	− 200
29	− 600	+ 600	+ 500	− 800	− 300
28	− 600	+ 600	+ 500	−1000	− 500
27	− 600	+ 600	+ 500	−1200	− 700
26	− 600	+ 600	+ 500	−1400	− 900

It can be opened long or short, using either calls or puts. There are four possible versions of a butterfly spread.

1. Sell two middle-range calls and buy one call above and one call below.
2. Sell two middle-range puts and buy one put above and one put below.

3. Buy two middle-range calls and sell one call above and one call below.
4. Buy two middle-range puts and sell one put above and one put below.

Example: You sell two June 30 calls for a premium of 5, and you buy one June 35 call at 1 and one June 25 call at 7. Your net proceeds are $200. Because this spread is a credit spread (you received more than you paid), you will gain a profit if the stock declines in value. And no matter how high the stock's price moves, the combined long position values will always exceed the two short positions.

Butterfly spreads are often created when one position is later expanded by the addition of other calls or puts. It is very difficult to find opportunities to create a riskless combination, especially one that will yield a credit to you.

Example: You previously sold two calls at a striking price of 30. The stock's value has declined to a point that the 25 calls are cheap, and you buy one to partially offset the short position. At the same time, you buy a 35 call, which is far out of the money.

The cost of commissions makes it difficult to open a butterfly spread and still maintain a credit. And the potential gain must be evaluated versus both commission costs and the risk of exercise.

Butterfly spreads can be created with either calls or puts and with either a bull or bear structure. A bull butterfly spread would be most profitable if the underlying stock increased in value, and a bear spread would be most profitable if the stock's value declined.

A detailed *butterfly spread*, with defined profit

butterfly spread: the opening of positions in one striking price range and offsetting them with transactions at higher and lower ranges (For example, two calls are sold while another is purchased with a higher striking price and another is purchased with a lower striking price. The buy/sell decision can be reversed, and the strategy can involve either calls or puts.)

and loss zones, is shown in Figure 8–14. In this example, you sell two June 40 calls at 6 (+$1200), and you buy one June 30 call at 12 (−$1200) and one June 50 call at 3 (−$300) at a net cost of $300. This butterfly spread strategy will either yield a limited profit or result in a limited loss. It consists of offsetting a position at one striking price with a higher and a lower position.

butterfly spread

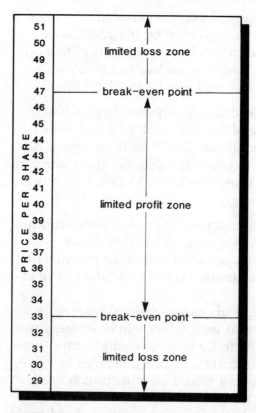

PRICE PER SHARE

51	
50	
49	limited loss zone
48	
47	break-even point
46	
45	
44	
43	
42	
41	
40	limited profit zone
39	
38	
37	
36	
35	
34	
33	break-even point
32	
31	limited loss zone
30	
29	

FIGURE 8–14. Butterfly Spread Profit and Loss Zones

As in many instances of the butterfly spread, the potential profit range is limited and too small to yield a profit after commissions. In this example, the potential profit and loss ranges involve three different exercise prices.

Table 8–D gives a summary of profits and losses at different prices of the underlying stock (assuming point of exercise and no remaining time value). If the stock rises to $50 or more, the

TABLE 8–D Profits/Losses for Butterfly Spread Example

Price	Jun 50	Jun 40	Jun 30	Total
$51	+ $900	− $1000	+ $100	0
50	+ 800	− 800	0	0
49	+ 700	− 600	− 300	− $200
48	+ 600	− 400	− 300	− 100
47	+ 500	− 200	− 300	0
46	+ 400	0	− 300	+ 100
45	+ 300	+ 200	− 300	+ 200
44	+ 200	+ 400	− 300	+ 300
43	+ 100	+ 600	− 300	+ 400
42	0	+ 800	− 300	+ 500
41	− 100	+ 1000	− 300	+ 600
40	− 200	+ 1200	− 300	+ 700
39	− 300	+ 1200	− 300	+ 600
38	− 400	+ 1200	− 300	+ 500
37	− 500	+ 1200	− 300	+ 400
36	− 600	+ 1200	− 300	+ 300
35	− 700	+ 1200	− 300	+ 200
34	− 800	+ 1200	− 300	+ 100
33	− 900	+ 1200	− 300	0
32	− 1000	+ 1200	− 300	− 100
31	− 1100	+ 1200	− 300	− 200
30	− 1200	+ 1200	− 300	− 300
29	− 1200	+ 1200	− 300	− 300
lower	− 1200	+ 1200	− 300	− 300

short positions are offset by an equal number of long positions. And if the stock declines, the maximum loss is $300, which is the cost of opening the butterfly spread.

UNDERSTANDING HEDGES

Whenever options are bought or sold as part of a strategy to protect another open position, the combined status is described as a hedge.

Long and Short Hedges

A long hedge protects you against price increases, while a short hedge is protection against price decreases.

Example of a *long hedge*: An investor is short on 100 shares of stock. He buys one call to protect the position in the event the stock's price increases.

Example of a *short hedge*: An investor is concerned about the possibility that a stock's value will decline. To hedge against this danger, there are two possible courses of action: buying one put for each 100 shares or selling one call for each 100 shares.

Long hedges protect investors by covering their short positions in the event of a price increase, the original and hedged positions offset one another. Short hedges are the opposite. They protect investors against price decreases that will adversely affect long positions.

An expanded example of a *long hedge*, with defined profit and loss zones, is shown in Figure 8–15. In this example, you sell short 100 shares at $43 per share, and you buy one May 40 call for 2 (−$200). This long hedge strategy assumes that the underlying stock's price has declined since purchase—to the point that the combined time and intrinsic value of a call is available for a premium of 2. With this assumption, you accept a reduced total profit potential to eliminate completely the risk of loss. The loss is eliminated only until the expiration date of the call, while the short position in stock may be kept open beyond that date.

If the underlying stock increases in value, the profit potential is limited to the comparative advantage between the stock and call value; it will never increase above that point spread. Increasing value in the short stock will be offset by the same degree in the long call. If the stock's value falls, the short stock position will be profitable, minus the two points paid for the call's protection.

Table 8–E gives a summary of the position's value as of expiration at various prices of the underlying stock.

long hedge: the purchase of options to protect a portfolio position in the event of a price increase, as a form of insurance (For example, an investor who is short 100 shares buys a call: If the stock's value rises, a corresponding rise in the call's premium will tend to offset losses.)

short hedge: the purchase of options to protect a portfolio position in the event of a price decrease, as a form of insurance (For example, an investor who is long 100 shares buys a put: If the stock declines in value, the increased value of the put will tend to offset losses.)

long hedge

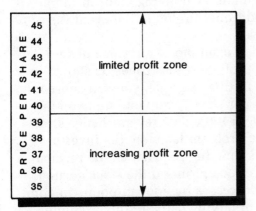

FIGURE 8–15. Long Hedge Profit and Loss Zones

TABLE 8–E Profits/Losses from the Long Hedge Example

Price	Stock	Call	Total
$45	− $200	+ $300	+ $100
44	100	+ 200	+ 100
43	0	+ 100	+ 100
42	+ 100	0	+ 100
41	+ 200	− 100	+ 100
40	+ 300	− 200	+ 100
39	+ 400	− 200	+ 200
38	+ 500	− 200	+ 300
37	+ 600	− 200	+ 400
36	+ 700	− 200	+ 500
35	+ 800	− 200	+ 600

Reverse Hedges

Hedges can be modified to increase potential profits or minimize the risk of loss.

A reverse hedge involves protecting a stock position to a greater degree than required. For example, you are short 100 shares of stock. You buy two calls, thereby providing twice the protection needed and also giving yourself the potential for additional profits in the event the stock does rise.

An expanded example of a *reverse hedge*, with defined profit and loss zones, is shown in Figure 8–16. In this example, you sell short 100 shares at $43 per share, and you buy two May 40 calls at 2 (− $400). This reverse hedge strategy solves the problem faced by the investor who utilizes a long hedge. That is, the reverse hedge will produce profits if the stock's value increases or decreases by enough points to eliminate the cost of buying calls. In this example, 100 shares were sold short at $43 per share, and

reverse hedge

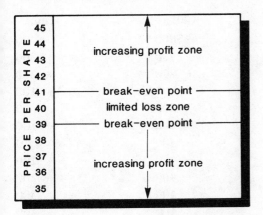

FIGURE 8–16. Reverse Hedge Profit and Loss Zones

two May 40 calls were bought. (Like the previous example, it must be assumed that the stock's price has declined since the short sale, so that the option's cost is not prohibitive.)

In this case, the reverse hedge creates its advantage in two ways: First, it protects the short position in the event of a price increase; second, the extra call adds profit potential to the position. And if the stock falls, the short position's profit potential is reduced by the cost of the calls.

Table 8–F gives a summary of the position's value as of expiration at various prices of the underlying stock.

Variable Hedges

Hedging can protect a long or short position in the underlying security, or it can reduce or eliminate risks in other option positions. Hedging is

variable hedge: a hedge between two related option positions, where one side involves more options than the other (For example, you buy three calls and sell one at a lower striking price. The difference in premium reduces the cost and might even result in cash proceeds, but the potential loss from the short call is offset by potential gains in the long calls.)

TABLE 8–F Profits/Losses from Reverse Hedge Example

Price	Stock	Call	Total
$45	− $200	+ $600	+ $400
44	100	+ 400	+ 300
43	0	+ 200	+ 200
42	+ 100	0	+ 100
41	+ 200	− 200	0
40	+ 300	− 400	− 100
39	+ 400	− 400	0
38	+ 500	− 400	+ 100
37	+ 600	− 400	+ 200
36	+ 700	− 400	+ 300
35	+ 800	− 400	+ 400

achieved with the various forms of spreads and combinations described in this chapter. And by varying the number of options on one side or the other, you create a variable hedge.

Example: You buy three May 60 calls and sell one May 55 call. If the price increases beyond the $60 per share level, your long position will increase by $3 for every $1 increase in the short position. If the stock falls, the short position can be closed at a profit.

Long and short *variable hedge* strategies with defined profit zones are illustrated in Figure 8–17. In the long variable hedge example, you buy three June 65 calls for 1 (− $300) and sell one June 60 call for 5 (+ $500), with net proceeds of $200. This long variable hedge strategy will achieve maximum profit if the underlying security rises in value. Above the striking price of $65 per share, the long calls will increase by $3 for each point in the stock, while the short position will offset only $1 per point. If the stock de-

variable hedge

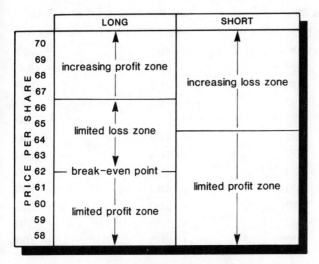

FIGURE 8–17. Variable Hedge Profit and Loss Zones

clines, all of the calls will lose value, and the proceeds of $200 will be profitable. Table 8–G gives a summary of this position's value as of expiration, at different stock prices.

In the short variable hedge example in Figure 8–17, you sell five June 60 calls for 5 (+ $2500) and buy three June 65 calls for 1 (− $300), with net proceeds of $2200. This short variable hedge strategy is a more aggressive form of variable hedge, with a higher level of proceeds and a correspondingly higher risk. When the offsetting call positions are eliminated, two calls are uncovered. A decline in the underlying stock's value will result in the entire $2200 being a profit. However, a rise in price will create an increasing level of losses. The outcomes of the short hedge at various stock prices as of expiration are given in Table 8–H.

TABLE 8–G Profits/Losses from the Long Variable Hedge Example

Price	Jun 60	Jun 65	Total
$70	+ $1200	− $500	+ $700
69	+ 900	− 400	+ 500
68	+ 600	− 300	+ 300
67	+ 300	− 200	+ 100
66	0	− 100	− 100
65	− 300	0	− 300
64	− 300	+ 100	− 200
63	− 300	+ 200	− 100
62	− 300	+ 300	0
61	− 300	+ 400	+ 100
60	− 300	+ 500	+ 200
59	− 300	+ 500	+ 200
58	− 300	+ 500	+ 200

TABLE 8–H Profits/Losses from the Short Variable Hedge Example

Price	Jun 60	Jun 65	Total
$70	− $2500	+ $500	− $1300
69	− 2000	+ 400	− 1100
68	− 1500	+ 300	− 900
67	− 1000	+ 200	− 700
66	− 500	0	− 500
65	0	− 300	− 300
64	+ 500	− 300	+ 200
63	+ 1000	− 300	+ 700
62	+ 1500	− 300	+ 1200
61	+ 2000	− 300	+ 1700
60	+ 2500	− 300	+ 2200
59	+ 2500	− 300	+ 2200
58	+ 2500	− 300	+ 2200

Ratio Write

Another form of hedging is the *ratio write*. A covered call writer is said to be 100 percent covered when one call is sold for every 100 shares of stock. A ratio write exists when the relationship between calls and shares of stock is higher or lower than one to one. See Table 8–I.

Example: You own 75 shares, and you sell a call. Strictly speaking, you own 75 shares long and have written one uncovered call. But when the potential losses are evaluated, the short position is 75 percent covered. The ratio write is 1 to ¾.

Example: You own 300 shares and sell four calls. You can view this strategy as three covered calls and one uncovered call, or you can call it a 4 to 3 ratio write.

An expanded example of the ratio write, with defined profit and loss zones, is shown in Figure 8–18. In this example, you buy 50 shares of stock at $38, and you sell one September 40 call for 3 (+$300). This ratio write strategy is a partially covered call. One-half of the risk in the short position is offset by the 50 calls held long.

ratio write: a relationship between long stock and short calls, other than one to one, that reduces risk on a portion of the total calls (For example, the owner of 400 shares sells five calls for a 5 to 4 ratio write involving four covered and one uncovered calls, or 80 percent coverage of the entire position.)

TABLE 8–I Ratio Writes

Calls Sold	Shares Owned	Percent Coverage	Ratio
1	75	75%	1 to 3/4
2	150	75	2 to 1 1/2
3	200	67	3 to 2
4	300	75	4 to 3
5	300	60	5 to 3
5	400	80	5 to 4

ratio write

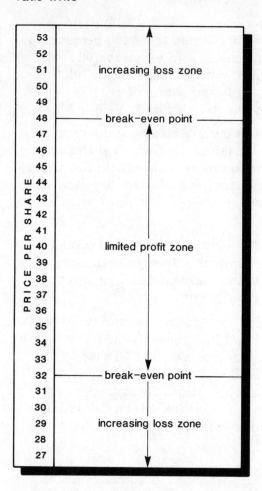

FIGURE 8–18. Ratio Write Profit and Loss Zones

If the value of the underlying stock increases, the degree of risk is cut in half by the shares. However, if the stock's price falls far enough, a loss in the stock will offset the premium received by selling the call. A summary of the

TABLE 8–J Profits/Losses from the Ratio Write Example

Price	Jul 40 Call	Jul 40 Put	Total
$50	+$600	−$700	−$100
49	+ 550	− 600	− 50
48	+ 500	− 500	0
47	+ 450	− 400	+ 50
46	+ 400	− 300	+ 100
45	+ 350	− 200	+ 150
44	+ 300	− 100	+ 200
43	+ 250	0	+ 250
42	+ 200	+ 100	+ 300
41	+ 150	+ 200	+ 350
40	+ 100	+ 300	+ 400
39	+ 50	+ 300	+ 350
38	0	+ 300	+ 300
37	− 50	+ 300	+ 250
36	− 100	+ 300	+ 200
35	− 150	+ 300	+ 150
34	− 200	+ 300	+ 100
33	− 250	+ 300	+ 50
32	− 300	+ 300	0
31	− 350	+ 300	− 50
30	− 400	+ 300	− 100

strategy, assuming various stock prices as of expiration, is given in Table 8–J.

UNDERSTANDING STRADDLES

While spreads involve buying and selling options with different terms, straddles are the simultaneous purchase and sale of options with the same striking price and expiration date.

long straddle: the purchase of the same number of calls and puts with identical striking prices and expiration dates (This strategy will be profitable if the stock's price moves above or below the striking price to a degree greater than the total cost of buying options.)

Long Straddle

A long straddle creates a middle loss zone and the potential for profit in the event of extreme price increases or decreases in the underlying stock.

Example: You buy one April 30 call for a premium of 2 and one April 30 put for a premium of 1. Your total cost is $300. As long as the price of the underlying stock remains within 3 points of the striking price, neither option will create a profit. The 3 points of intrinsic value is equal to your net cost. However, once the price is higher or lower by more than 3 points, the long straddle will be profitable.

An example of a *long straddle*, with defined profit and loss zones, is illustrated in Figure 8–19. In this example, you buy one July 40 call

long straddle

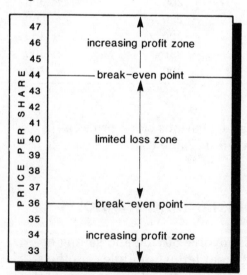

FIGURE 8–19. Long Straddle Profit and Loss Zones

for 3 (− $300) and one July 40 put for 1 (− $100) at a net cost of $400. This long straddle strategy involves assuming a long position in calls and puts of the same stock, with the same striking price and expiration date. It will become profitable if the underlying stock's price movement is substantial enough in either direction to exceed the cost of opening the position. Table 8–K gives a summary of the outcomes at various stock prices as of expiration.

short straddle: the sale of the same number of calls and puts with identical striking prices and expiration dates (This strategy will be profitable if the stock's price does not move away from the striking price to a degree greater than the proceeds received by the investor.)

Short Straddle

A short straddle involves selling a call and a put with the same expiration date and striking price. This action creates a middle ground for both potential profits as well as the risk of losses if the

TABLE 8–K Profits/Losses from the Long Straddle Example

Price	Jul 40 Call	Jul 40 Put	Total
$47	+ $400	− $100	+ $300
46	+ 300	− 100	+ 200
45	+ 200	− 100	+ 100
44	+ 100	− 100	0
43	0	− 100	− 100
42	− 100	− 100	− 200
41	− 200	− 100	− 300
40	− 300	− 100	− 400
39	− 300	0	− 300
38	− 300	+ 100	− 200
37	− 300	+ 200	− 100
36	− 300	+ 300	0
35	− 300	+ 400	+ 100
34	− 300	+ 500	+ 200
33	− 300	+ 600	+ 300

underlying stock exceeds that range on either side.

Example: You sell an April 30 call for 2 and an April 30 put for 1. You receive a total of $300. As long as the price remains within 3 points of the striking price, any intrinsic value in the options will be offset by the amount you received. If the underlying stock's price exceeds the profit zone by 3 points or more, the short straddle will result in a loss.

An example of the *short straddle* strategy, with defined profit and loss zones, is shown in Figure 8–20. In this example, you sell one July 40 call for 3 (+$300) and one July 40 put for 1 (+$100), with net proceeds of $400. This short straddle strategy is exactly opposite of the long straddle. In this case, the position consists of

short straddle

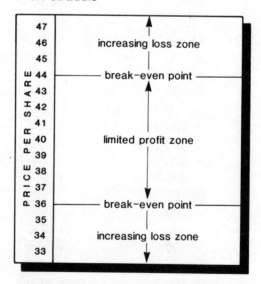

FIGURE 8–20. Short Straddle Profit and Loss Zones

two short positions, one each in the call and the put of the same underlying security with the same striking price and expiration date. As long as the underlying stock's value remains within a range above or below the striking price, a profit will result. In this example, that range is 4 points (proceeds of selling the options). Unless the expiration price is equal to the striking price, or the position is closed before expiration, either the call or the put will be exercised. Table 8–L gives a summary of the short straddle's outcomes, given various stock prices as of expiration.

Actual profits and losses must be adjusted to allow for the cost of commissions upon opening and closing the straddle. With either the long or the short straddle strategy the higher the cost of

TABLE 8–L Profits/Losses from the Short Straddle Example

Price	Jul 40 Call	Jul 40 Put	Total
$47	− $400	+ $100	− $300
46	− 300	+ 100	− 200
45	− 200	+ 100	− 100
44	− 100	+ 100	0
43	0	+ 100	+ 100
42	+ 100	+ 100	+ 200
41	+ 200	+ 100	+ 300
40	+ 300	+ 100	+ 400
39	+ 300	0	+ 300
38	+ 300	− 100	+ 200
37	+ 300	− 200	+ 100
36	+ 300	− 300	0
35	+ 300	− 400	− 100
34	+ 300	− 500	− 200
33	+ 300	− 600	− 300

long and short straddle

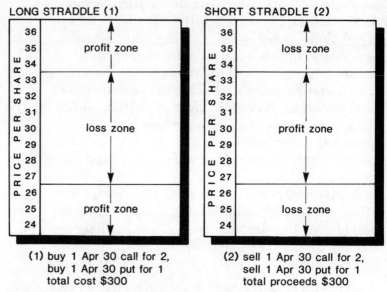

LONG STRADDLE (1)

SHORT STRADDLE (2)

(1) buy 1 Apr 30 call for 2,
buy 1 Apr 30 put for 1
total cost $300

(2) sell 1 Apr 30 call for 2,
sell 1 Apr 30 put for 1
total proceeds $300

FIGURE 8–21. Comparison of Long and Short Straddle Strategies

purchased options or the lower the cost of sold options, the lower is the chances for profit. See Figure 8–21.

USING COMBINED TECHNIQUES THEORY AND PRACTICE

Advanced option strategies expose you to danger, especially when short positions are involved. If you decide to attempt any of these ideas in your own portfolio, you should remember the following points.

1. Commissions will reduce profit margins and extend potential loss zones. This cost must be added to estimated purchase prices and subtracted from estimated sales.

2. A buyer has the right to exercise a call or a put at any time. Never assume that options can be exercised only on the last day of the cycle.

3. Always evaluate a strategy in terms of potential reward versus your risks.

4. Taking short positions will result in your being required to meet minimum margin requirements, which means you must have the commitment of cash or securities in your brokerage account.

5. No strategy should be employed until you understand all of the risks involved and have identified appropriate actions in the event of price movement.

6. An option strategy might seem simple and safe on paper, but in practice could prove much more involved. Only experience will reveal the extent of difference between theory and practice in option trading. But be aware that sudden changes in the price of the underlying stock, in the market in general, and in the demand for options, all can affect profitability.

9

Choosing Your Own Strategy

The successful investor controls a portfolio by first defining risk standards and then determining what to buy and sell. Whether you define your standards as speculative, conservative, or somewhere in between, options might provide a valuable form of diversification, protection, or income opportunities.

A speculative investor will favor the income opportunities in selling uncovered options and is willing to take risks. Or this investor will use spreads and straddles to profit while minimizing losses. Speculators can also hedge their risk positions by purchasing options to offset potential portfolio losses.

The conservative investor seeking income rather than long-term growth will be willing to accept a consistently high rate of return by selling covered calls. To protect the value of long positions, the very conservative investor will benefit from buying puts. In the event of a decline in the stock's value, the put serves as insurance against loss. Investors seeking short-term income but unwilling to accept unlimited risks will concentrate on buying calls and puts.

KNOWING THE RANGE OF RISK

Options serve the entire spectrum of risk profiles and can be used to speculate or to insure the value of stock. In order to identify how options can best serve your personal investing requirements, you must take three steps.

1. Become thoroughly knowledgeable about the techniques of option investing.
2. Identify your own investing standards and goals.
3. Identify the specific risks of options, including the contingent risks beyond unexpected price movement.

The obvious risk for any option position is that the underlying stock will move in a direction opposite of what you expect. This danger is accepted by the speculator who seeks immediate income and by the conservative investor who uses options to lock in a rate of return or to insure the value of a position.

Beyond these, six other forms of risk must be acknowledged by every option investor: margin, personal goal, unavailability of a market, disruption in trading, brokerage, and commission risks.

Margin Risks

Most investors think of margin investing as buying stocks on credit. But in the options market,

the margin requirement is different. Your broker
will require that any short position in options
must be protected with collateral.

Cash or securities must be deposited to protect a portion of the value when you assume a
short position. For example, an investor who
sells uncovered calls will be required to maintain a specific level of value in the brokerage account. The balance is at risk. So if the stock's
value increases, the margin requirement will increase, too.

The risk is that in the event of unexpected
changes in value of the underlying stock, you
will be required to deposit additional money or
securities to meet the margin requirement. Before entering into a position involving uncovered
calls or puts, spreads, or straddles, you should
discuss margin requirements with your broker
and be certain that you can afford to meet those
requirements.

Personal Goal Risks

You must set investing standards for yourself
and establish rules you will follow consistently.
If you do not take this step, your chances for
profits from option trading will be reduced.

Example: You start out with the idea that you
will use no more than 10 percent of your total
portfolio to speculate in options. You buy calls
and puts and earn respectable profits. At this
point, it is easy to lose sight of your original intention and put a higher portion of your portfolio into options. As a result, you could lose more
money than you can afford. By not respecting
your own standards, you increase the risk.

Your standards should include identifying the point where you will close an open position. Avoid breaking your own rules by delaying action in the hope for greater profits in the future. Establish two points: *minimum gain* and *maximum loss*. When either point is reached, close your positions.

Unavailability of a Market Risk

A discussion of any option strategy assumes that you will be able to open and close positions whenever you want. Timing is the essential element of all option trades. But as an option investor, you must accept the continuous risk that a market could be unavailable for a number of reasons.

Example: On October 19, 1987, the stock market experienced the worst decline to that point in its history. Volume exceeded 600 million shares, and brokerage firms fell several days behind in completing orders. Investors were unable to reach their brokers by telephone, and even orders already placed were delayed several days. During the following week, prices of stocks moved through a wide range of values. Option investors, notably speculators, suffered tremendous losses in many instances. And they were unable to cut their losses by immediately placing a closing transaction—the market was not available.

The same problem can occur if an exchange halts trading options on a particular stock or ceases trading options altogether for a period of days. The exchanges cannot guarantee a prompt and continuous market.

Disruption in Trading Risks

Another risk is that trading will be halted in the underlying stock. When that occurs, trading in related options will also be halted. This situation presents a particularly severe risk for speculators.

Example: You sell an uncovered call and receive a premium with very high time value. A few days later, a tender offer is made on the stock $20 above the striking price. The exchange halts trading. You cannot close the position and limit your losses or buy stock to cover your position.

In the same circumstances, a call buyer will not be able to close a position and take profits, until trading is resumed. By that time, the rumor might have been denied, and the underlying stock's value could be back where it started.

In some situations, option buyers will be able to exercise even when trading has been halted. But in such circumstances, you will have to exercise without knowing the value of the underlying stock.

Brokerage Risks

If your brokerage firm becomes insolvent or if a regulatory agency takes over operation, you might be unable to close open positions at will. Or your positions might be closed without your authorization to eliminate risks of losses to the firm itself.

In the event of widespread brokerage insolvency, the Options Clearing Corporation would not necessarily be able to honor the exercise of all option contracts. The system of margin requirements and limitations on individual option positions in effect limits this risk. But every option investor must recognize that it exists.

Another form of brokerage risk involves the conduct of your personal broker. You should never grant unlimited trading discretion to a broker, no matter how much trust you have. Option trading, with its varied and special risks, is not appropriate in every form for every investor. There have been incidents of broker abuse in the past, and there probably will be again in the future. Unfortunately, when too much trust is placed in a broker, the problem is not discovered until after losses have occurred. It's a mistake to allow a broker, by virtue of experience or knowledge, to dictate positions in options or any other security without your consent and outside of your control.

Commission Risks

A calculated profit zone must be reduced to allow for the cost of trading. And a loss zone must be expanded for the same reason. Trading single options reduces the amount of money at risk, but also increases the per-option cost.

You risk losing sight of the cost of trading, so that marginally profitable trades on a precommission basis actually result in small losses. For the overall risk assumed, you might realize little or nothing for your efforts. Always calculate the risk and potential for profit with trading costs in mind.

EVALUATING YOUR RISK TOLERANCE

Every investor has a specific level of risk tolerance, or ability and willingness to accept risks.

The degree of tolerance depends on a number of factors.

- Amount of money the investor has available for speculative investments
- Age, income, and economic status of the investor
- Investor's level of knowledge of and experience with a particular type of investment
- Type of trading account the investor has (For example, in IRA and Keogh accounts, only one form of option trading—covered call writing—is allowed, although in some of these accounts, investors might also be allowed to purchase puts to hedge a position.)
- Investor's personal objectives, such as the desire to protect value through conservative investing, short-term income through speculation, consistent rate of return, long-term growth, or a percentage distribution of different objectives.

Some investors split their portfolios into distinct segments. One part is left in long-term growth investments, while another is put into more aggressive income funds or stocks. A small portion might be used for more speculative investments like the purchase of options.

Whatever profile fits you, it should be well understood before any investment is made. Rather than depending on the advice of a broker, the financial rumors or news you read in the paper, or other isolated indicators and trends, be sure you invest with your risk tolerance in mind. That should be the force that guides every decision you make as an investor.

The best decisions are those made after evaluating risks. By putting down on paper the types of available option trades, you will gain a clear view of how options can fit into your portfolio. The evaluation process will also help you to avoid including options when they are not appropriate—given the risk tolerance you assign to yourself.

The risk evaluation worksheet for option investing shown in Table 9–A will help you to classify options in categories of risk.

Applying Limits

Awareness of your own limits must guide all option activities in your portfolio. Whenever you hold an open position, you must understand not only your goal and risk tolerance, but also the target rate of return you expect—or the degree of loss you are willing to accept.

To define these limits, identify option trades you will make by the rate of return and features of the option. For example, covered call sellers should always identify the potential return in selling calls if the stock is unchanged and if the option is exercised.

Option purchasers should evaluate what they will buy on these points.

1. *Maximum time value:* As a standard, buy only those options whose premiums do not contain an excessive level of time value. Time works against you as a buyer, and all of the time value will disappear by expiration date. The level you pick will also dictate how close to the money you will eventually purchase options.

Example: You decide that options should contain no more than 50 percent time value. If the

TABLE 9–A Risk Evaluation Worksheet

Lowest possible risk

_____ Covered call writing

_____ Put purchase for insurance
(long position)

_____ Call purchase for insurance
(short position)

Medium risk

_____ Ratio writing

_____ Combined strategies
_____ long _____ short

High risk

_____ Uncovered call writing

_____ Combined strategies
_____ long _____ short

_____ Call purchases for income

_____ Put purchases for income

option's total premium is 3 ($300), you thus require that no more than 1 ½ points of time value are involved. In this case, you will always buy options at least 1 ½ points in the money.

2. *Time until expiration:* Buyers of very short-term options will be fortunate to realize a profit. That depends on enough movement in the underlying stock to increase intrinsic value of the call or put. So you need some time in order to build intrinsic profits. Decide in advance how many months you consider "ideal": enough time to allow for price movement, but not so much that you pay for an excessive level of time value.

Example: You want to minimize time value premium, but also want at least two months until expiration date. The goal of maximum time value must be coordinated with a realistic goal for expiration time. You decide to not purchase any options that do not have at least two months until expiration date.

3. *Number of options:* You must also decide how many options to buy in one trade. If you buy several contracts, the commission cost is greatly reduced, but if the move is not profitable, you also stand to lose more money.

Example: The fee for trading options with one discount broker for trades of $2000 or less is $18 plus 1.8 percent of the premium. Cost varies depending on the number of options traded at one time:

- One option, premium of 3 ($300) $23.40
- Two options, premium of 3 ($600)   28.80
- Three options, premium of 3 ($900)   34.20

For three options, the commission cost is $11.40 per contract or less than half the fee for a single contract.

4. *Target rate of return:* Enter every option trade with a goal for the rate of return. Identify this goal in advance.

Example: You buy options at 3 ($300) or less with the goal of netting a profit of 50 percent or more. Whenever the premium value increases by 50 percent or more (adjusted for commissions), the position is closed.

5. *Buy and sell levels:* Along with a target rate of return, identify the premium level at which you will close the position. Respect this level. When premiums rise (for long positions) or fall (for short positions) to your target price, close the position. And, to minimize losses, also close if you reach an identified bail-out point.

Example: You buy options in groups of three, with a maximum price range of 3 ($300) per contract, and you set the following standard: If the value increases to $450 or if it decreases to $150, the positions will be closed.

By identifying all of the features you consider minimally acceptable and all of the risks you are willing to assume, you then are able to select those options that fit your limits. If your limits are unrealistic, no options will be available.

Example: You decide you will buy options with no more than 25 percent time value premium, with at least six months until expiration, and that are at the money. You will never find this combination. With that many months until expiration, time value will usually be greater. You will have to buy long-term calls deeper out of the money or accept a higher level of time value.

When considering an option strategy, you should first calculate potential profits in the events of expiration and exercise and then set criteria for other points: Maximum time value, time until expiration, number of contracts, target rate of return, and the price range in which you will sell. Use the Option Limits Worksheet shown in Table 9–B to set your limits. Then, respect the limits you set. By deciding in advance the characteristics of your option investment and by knowing when you will sell, you will avoid the common problem of investing in a void.

TABLE 9–B Option Limits

Covered Call Sale Criteria

Rate of Return if Unchanged
Dividends	$ _____		
Call premium	_____	Total	$ _____
		Cost of Stock	$ _____
		Gain	_____ %

Rate of Return if Exercised
Dividends	$ _____		
Call premium	_____		
Stock gain	_____	Total	$ _____
		Cost of stock	$ _____
		Gain	_____ %

Option Purchase Criteria

Maximum time value: _____ %

Time until expiration: _____ months

Number of options: _____ contracts

Target rate of return: _____ %

Sell level: increase to $ _____ or decrease to $ _____

Many people have invested wisely at first, only to fail by not closing their positions at the right moment.

LOOKING TO THE FUTURE

Besides setting immediate standards and goals for option strategies in your portfolio, set long-term investing policies. Then fit option strategies into those policies.

It's a mistake to open an option position on the advice of a broker or adviser without first considering how that fits into your long-term investing policy. Options must be used in an appropriate context.

Example: You want to build the value of your portfolio over time and are willing to assume low-to-moderate risks. So you put your money into shares of blue chip companies. In order to increase value over time, you consider one of two policies.

Policy 1: Hold the shares of stock as long-term investments. After many years, the accumulation of well-selected companies will increase the value of the investments, and current dividends will provide income.

Policy 2: Increase the value of your portfolio by purchasing shares and writing covered calls. Income from (a) profitable turnover through exercise, (b) call premiums, and (c) on-going dividends will all be reinvested in a growing number of shares with several blue-chip companies.

In this example, the rate of return with Policy 2 will be greater due to the consistently high yield from selling calls. The return includes a discount for the purchase price and an increase for the amount of cash available to invest.

The long-term goal of building a portfolio's value can be achieved by using options in an appropriate way. You will give up the yields that might be earned if a company's stock jumps unexpectedly in value because selling calls locks in a striking price. But remembering that the goal is steady long-term growth, anticipating the possibility of sudden price swings is not applicable in either Policy 1 or Policy 2.

An impatient investor might be tempted to take a speculative approach, perhaps by buying options instead of stock. If the options are consistently profitable, you could achieve the goal of increasing value in a few months instead of having to wait several years. But the chances of loss are high, and this approach is contrary to your long-term goals.

Like any form of investing, options can be applied to your goals and risk standards and used intelligently to create profits, hedge against losses, or discount the price of stock purchases. Investors who lose in the options market fail to set their goals and do not select strategies appropriate for their financial status or long-range plans and intentions.

Success must be based on knowledge, research, discipline, and, to an extent, experimentation. You cannot learn all that you need to know about trading in any investment without actually commiting funds and assuming a risk, even a limited one.

Devising a strategy with which you are comfortable and then seeing it work is a rewarding experience. Not only will you profit from a well-planned and appropriate use of options, you will also enjoy the satisfaction of mastering a complex investment and knowing that you are in control.

Glossary

assignment the act of exercise against a seller (When the buyer exercises an option, it is assigned to a seller usually on a random basis.)

at the money a condition in which the market value of the underlying security is identical to the striking price of the option

automatic exercise action taken by the Options Clearing Corporation at the time of expiration, when an in-the-money option has not been otherwise exercised or canceled

average down a technique for absorbing paper losses on stock investments (By buying shares periodically, the average price is higher than current market value, but part of the paper loss is absorbed on average, thereby enabling covered call writers to profit even when the stock has declined in value.)

average up a technique for buying stocks when the market value is increasing (By buying shares periodically, the average price is consistently lower than current market value, thereby enabling the covered

buy 100 shares per month:

MONTH	PRICE	AVERAGE
Jan	$40	$40
Feb	38	39
Mar	36	38
Apr	34	37
May	27	35
Jun	29	34

FIGURE G.1. Average Down

buy 100 shares per month:

MONTH	PRICE	AVERAGE
Jan	$40	$40
Feb	44	42
Mar	45	43
Apr	47	44
May	54	46
Jun	52	47

FIGURE G.2. Average Up

call writer to sell in-the-money calls when the overall basis in stock is lower than a desirable striking price.)

bear spread the purchase and sale of calls or puts that will create maximum profits when the value of the underlying security falls (Options with a higher striking price are bought, and an equal number of options with a lower striking price are sold.)

beta a measurement of the relative volatility of a stock, made by comparing the degree of price movement to movement in an overall index

box spread the opening of a bull spread and a bear spread at the same time and on the same underlying stock (The investor will maximize profits when the stock rises or falls in value.)

break-even price (also called break-even point) the price of the underlying stock at which the option investor breaks even (For the call buyer, this price amounts to the number of points above the striking price of the stock that equals price of the call before allowing for commission costs.)

bull spread the purchase and sale of calls or puts that will create maximum profits when the value of the underlying security rises (Options with a lower striking price are bought, and an equal number of options with a higher striking price are sold.)

butterfly spread the opening of positions in one striking price range and offsetting them with transactions at higher and lower ranges (For example, two calls are sold while another is purchased with a higher striking price and another is purchased with a lower striking price. The buy/sell decision can be reversed, and the strategy can involve either calls or puts.)

buyer an investor who purchases a call or a put option (If the value of the option rises, the buyer will realize a profit by selling the option at a price above the purchase price.)

calendar spread a strategy in which options bought and sold on the same underlying stock have different expiration dates

call an option acquired by a buyer or granted by a seller to buy 100 shares of stock at a fixed price

called away the result of having stock assigned (For each call option exercised, 100 shares of the seller's stock are called away at the striking price.)

class all options traded on a single underlying security, including different striking prices and expiration dates

closed position the status of an option that has been canceled or exercised or is expired

closing purchase transaction a purchase to close a previous short position (For example, if you previously sold an option, a closing purchase transaction cancels that position.)

closing sale transaction a sale to close a previous long position (For example, if you previously bought an option, a closing sale transaction cancels that position.)

combination any multiple purchase and/or sale of related securities whose terms are not identical

contract a single option, including the attributes of that option: identification of the stock on which it is written, the cost of the option, date the option will expire, and the fixed price at which the stock will be bought or sold if the option is exercised

conversion the process of moving assigned stock from the seller of a call option or to the seller of a put option (Ownership is converted through the buyer's exercise of the option.)

cover descriptive of the status when an investor is long in the stock and short in a call option (For each option contract sold, the investor owns 100 shares.)

covered option a call option that is sold to create an open position, when the investor has 100 shares to cover the short option position

credit spread any spread in which the receipts from short positions exceed the cost of long positions (For example, a May 40 call is sold for a premium of 6 and a May 45 call is bought for a premium of 1, with a net credit of 5 ($500) before commissions.)

current market value the market value of stock at the present time

cycle the series of expiration dates on the options of a particular underlying stock (There are three cycles, according to expiration dates: (1) January, April, July, and October; (2) February, May, August, and November; and (3) March, June, September, and December.)

debit spread any spread in which the receipts from short positions are less than the cost of long positions

(For example, a June 55 call is sold for a premium of 2 and a June 50 call is bought for a premium of 6, with a net debit of 4 ($400).

deep in/deep out terms describing an option when the underlying stock is more than 5 points above or 5 points below the striking price.

SHARE PRICE	CALLS	PUTS
48		
47	deep in	deep out
46		
45	- - - - - -	- - - - - -
44	in the	out of the
43	money	money
42		
41		
40	— striking price —	
39		
38	out of the	in the
37	money	money
36		
35	- - - - - -	- - - - - -
34		
33	deep out	deep in
32		

FIGURE G.3. Deep in/Deep out

delivery physical movement of stock from one owner to another (Shares are transferred upon registration of stock to the new owner and payment of the market value of those shares.)

delta the relationship of change in an option's premium to changes in the price of the underlying stock (When the two move the same number of points, the delta is 1.00; a higher or lower delta can act as a signal to take advantage of adjustments in time value.)

diagonal spread a calender spread in which the offsetting options have both different striking prices and different expiration dates

discount a benefit of selling covered calls (The true price of the stock is reduced by the amount of pre-

stock price change	OPTION PREMIUM CHANGE			
	1 point	2 points	3 points	4 points
1	1.00	2.00	3.00	4.00
2	0.50	1.00	1.50	2.00
3	0.33	0.67	1.00	1.33
4	0.25	0.50	0.75	1.00
5	0.20	0.40	0.60	0.80

FIGURE G.4. Delta

mium received: If the basis in stock is $30 per share and an option is sold for a premium of 5, the basis is discounted to $25 per share.)

downside protection a strategy involving the purchase of one put for every 100 shares owned, as a form of insurance (Every point drop in the stock is matched by an increase of 1 point in the put.)

early exercise the act of exercising an option prior to expiration date (Buyers have the right to exercise at any time.)

exercise the act of buying or selling stock at the fixed price specified in the option contract (When a buyer exercises an option, he or she purchases stock at a price lower than market value; when a put is exercised, he or she sells stock at a price higher than market value.)

expiration date the date that an option becomes worthless (Every option contract includes a specified date in the future on which it expires.)

expiration time the latest possible time to place an order for cancellation or exercise, which is 5:30 P.M. (New York time) on the Friday immediately preceding the third Saturday of the expiration month

fundamental analysis the study of financial aspects of a company or industry to determine the safety and value of an investment (Fundamentalists believe that future value is determined by historical profits, dividend yield, the P/E ratio, and other financial trends.)

hedge a strategy in which one position protects the other (Buying a put is a form of hedge to protect the value of 100 shares of the underlying stock.)

horizontal spread a calender spread in which the offsetting options have the same striking price but different expiration dates

incremental return a technique of avoiding exercise when the value of the underlying stock is rising (One call position is closed at a loss, but replaced by two or more new call positions; the net effect of this is to produce a cash profit.)

in the money a condition in which the market value of the underlying stock is higher than the call's striking price or lower than the put's striking price

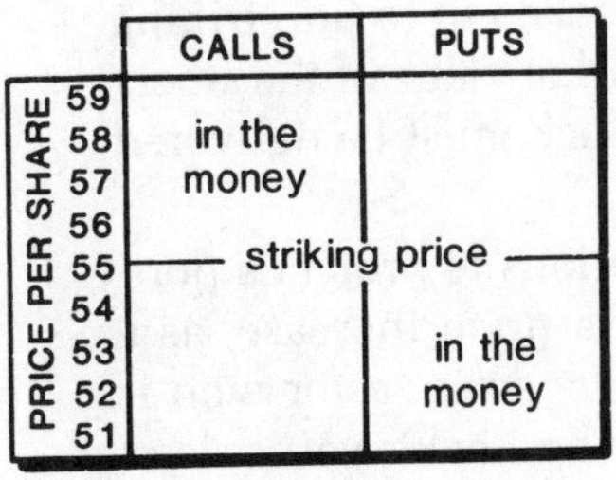

	CALLS	PUTS
59	in the	
58	money	
57		
56		
55	— striking price —	
54		
53		in the
52		money
51		

PRICE PER SHARE

FIGURE G.5. In the Money

intrinsic value the amount the option is in the money (An at-the-money or out-of-the-money option has no intrinsic value.)

last trading day the Friday preceding third Saturday of the expiration month of an option

leverage the use of a limited amount of money to control greater values (A call buyer who spends $300 to control $5000 worth of stock has more leverage than an investor who spends $5000 to buy 100 shares.)

STOCK VALUE	STRIKING PRICE	INTRINSIC VALUE
$38	$35	$3
43	45	0
41	40	1
65	65	0
21	20	1

FIGURE G.6. Intrinsic Value

listed option an option traded on a public exchange (Listed options are traded on the New York, Chicago, Pacific, American, and Philadelphia stock exchanges.)

lock in condition of the underlying security when the investor has an offsetting short call (As long as the call is open, the writer is locked in to the striking price, regardless of current market value of the stock; in the event of exercise, the stock must be delivered at that locked in price.)

long hedge the purchase of options to protect a portfolio position in the event of a price increase, as a form of insurance (For example, an investor who is short 100 shares buys a call: If the stock's value rises, a corresponding rise in the call's premium will tend to offset losses.)

long position the status of any investment that has been bought and is currently held, pending an offsetting sale (to cancel the position) or expiration

long straddle the purchase of the same number of calls and puts with identical striking prices and expiration dates (This strategy will be profitable if the stock's price moves above or below the striking price to a degree greater than the total cost of buying options.)

loss zone the price range of the underlying stock in which the option investor will lose (A limited loss occurs for a call buyer between the striking price and the break-even price; otherwise, the loss zone is any stock price lower than the option's striking price.)

margin an account with a brokerage firm that contains a minimum, required amount of cash or securities to provide collateral for short positions or for purchases made and not paid for until sold.

market value the value of an investment as of a specified time or date, or the price that buyers are willing to pay and sellers are willing to receive for a stock or option

married put descriptive of a hedge position when a put and 100 shares are bought at the same time (The put is "married" to the 100 shares on which the downside protection is provided.)

money spread another term for the vertical spread

naked option an option that is sold to create an open position, when the seller does not own 100 shares of the underlying stock

naked option

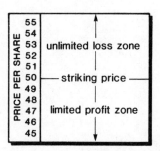

FIGURE G.7. Naked Option

naked position the status when the seller does not own 100 shares of the underlying stock, but has sold a call

opening purchase transaction a transaction executed to buy, also known as "going long"

opening sale transaction a transaction executed to sell, also known as "going short"

open interest the number of open contracts on a particular option (Increases in open interest reflect the *total* contracts outstanding, but do not show whether volume is due to increased activity among buyers or sellers.)

open position the status when a purchase (long) transaction or a sale (short) transaction has been made (The position remains open until cancellation, expiration, or exercise.)

option the right to buy or sell 100 shares of stock at a fixed price and by a specified date

out of the money (the opposite of "in the money") a condition in which the market value of the underlying stock is lower than the call's striking price or higher than the put's striking price

PRICE PER SHARE	CALLS	PUTS
59		
58		out of the
57		money
56		
55	— striking price —	
54		
53	out of the	
52	money	
51		

FIGURE G.8. Out of the Money

paper profit or loss (also called unrealized profits or losses) values that exist only because current market value is higher or lower than the investor's basis (These profits or losses can be realized—taken—only by closing the position.)

parity the condition of an option when the total premium is identical to intrinsic value and no time value exists

premium the current price of an option, which buyers pay and sellers receive at the time of the transaction (The amount is expressed as the amount per share, without dollar signs; for example, when a broker states that an option "is at 3," that means its premium is $300.)

profit zone the price range of the underlying stock in which the option investor will realize a profit (For a call buyer, the profit zone extends upward from the break-even price.)

put an option acquired by a buyer or granted by a seller to sell 100 shares of stock at a fixed price

put to seller the action that occurs when a put buyer exercises the put (The 100 shares of stock are sold —put—to the seller at the striking price.

ratio calendar combination a spread strategy involving both a ratio between purchases and sales and a box spread (Long and short positions are opened in the same security but in varying numbers of contracts and with expiration dates extending over two or more periods in order to produce profits during periods of price increases or decreases in the underlying stock.)

ratio calendar spread a spread strategy in which the number of options bought is different from the number that are sold and in which the expiration dates of the options on each side differ (This strategy establishes two profit/loss zones, one of which disappears upon the earlier expiration.)

ratio write a relationship between long stock and short calls, other than one to one, that reduces risk on a portion of the total calls. (For example, the owner of 400 shares sells 5 calls for a 5 to 4 ratio write involving four covered and one uncovered calls or 80% coverage of the entire position.

realized profit or loss profits or losses that are taken when an investor closes a position

return if exercised the estimated rate of return an option seller will earn in the event of exercise (The calculation includes profit on the purchase and sale of the underlying stock, dividends, and premium received.)

```
exercise price 40
purchase price 38
May 40 call sold for 3
dividends earned $80
```

call premium	$300
dividend income	80
capital gain	200
return	$580
	15.3%

FIGURE G.9. Return if Exercised

return if unchanged the estimated rate of return an option seller will earn if the option is not exercised (The assumption is that the stock will remain out of the money until expiration, so that the return will consist of the call premium and any dividends earned on the underlying stock.)

```
basis in stock   $3,800
```

sold May 40 call	$300
dividends earned	80
total	$380
return	10.0%

FIGURE G.10. Return if Unchanged

reverse hedge an extension of a long or short hedge in which more options are purchased than needed to provide insurance (For example, an investor is short 200 shares, and buys three calls: If the price rises, every 2 points of loss on the short stock position will be offset by 3 points of gain in the calls.)

roll down the replacement of one call with another that has a lower striking price

roll forward the replacement of one call with a call that has the same striking price, but a later expiration date

roll up the replacement of one call with a call that has a higher striking price

seller an investor who sells an option (If the value of the option falls, the buyer will realize a profit by buying, or canceling, the option at a price below the original sales price.)

series a group of options sharing identical terms

settlement date the date on which an investor must pay for purchases or is paid for sales (Stock settlement occurs five business days after the transaction date; option settlement occurs on the business day following the transaction.)

short hedge the purchase of options to protect a portfolio position in the event of a price decrease, as a form of insurance (For example, an investor who is long 100 shares buys a put: If the stock declines in value, the increased value of the put will tend to offset losses.)

short position the status of any investment that has been sold and is currently held, pending an offsetting purchase (to cancel the position) or expiration

short straddle the sale of the same number of calls and puts with identical striking prices and expiration dates (This strategy will be profitable if the stock's price does not move away from the striking price to a degree greater than the proceeds received by the investor.)

speculation a risky use of money to create immediate or short-term profits, with the knowledge that substantial or total losses are also likely (Buying calls for leverage is a form of speculation: The buyer might earn a large profit in a short period of time or lose the entire premium.)

spread the simultaneous purchase and sale of options—on the same underlying stock—with different striking price or expiration dates or both (The purpose is to increase potential for profits, while reducing risks if the underlying stock's movement exceeds what is anticipated, or to take advantage of the timing of stock price movement.)

straddle the simultaneous purchase and sale of the same number of calls and puts with identical striking prices and expiration dates

striking price the price of stock indicated in the option contract (For example, when an option specifies a striking price of $45 per share, regardless of the actual market value of the stock, that option can be exercised at the striking price of $45 per share.)

suitability a standard by which an investment or market strategy is judged (The investor's knowledge and experience in options is an important suitability standard, and a strategy is appropriate only if the investor can afford the risks that are involved.)

tax put a strategy involving the sale of stock at a loss—taken for tax purposes—and the sale of a put (The premium on the put eliminates the loss on sale of stock: If exercised, the investor buys back the stock at the striking price.

technical analysis the study of trends and statistics in the market to identify buying and selling opportunities (Technicians believe that price movement is predictable based on historical patterns and trends.)

terms the complete description of an option, including the underlying security, type (call or put), striking price, and expiration month

time spread another term for a calendar spread

time value the option's premium above any intrinsic value (When an option is at the money or out of the money, the entire premium represents time value.)

TOTAL PREMIUM	INTRINSIC VALUE	TIME VALUE
$4	$3	$1
2	0	2
4	1	3
1	0	1
3	1	2

FIGURE G.11. Time Value

total return the combination of income from the call premium, capital gains in the stock, and any dividends received (Total return should be computed in two ways: if the option is exercised and if it expires worthless.)

stock exercised at
$40 (basis $34),
held for 13 months:

option premium	$ 800
dividends	110
capital gain	600
total	$1,510
13 months	44.4%
annualized	41.0%

FIGURE G.12. Total Return

uncovered option the same as a naked option, or the opposite of a covered option (when a call is sold and the investor also owns 100 shares)

underlying stock (also called underlying security) the stock on which the option grants rights to buy or sell (Every stock option refers to a specific, underlying stock.)

variable hedge a hedge between two related option positions, where one side involves more options than the other (For example, you buy three calls and sell one at a lower striking price. The difference in premium reduces the cost and might even result in cash proceeds, but the potential loss from the short call is offset by potential gains in the long calls.)

vertical spread any bull or bear spread that involves options with different striking prices, but identical expiration dates

volatility a measure of the degree of change in a stock's market price during a twelve-month period, stated as a percentage (To compute, subtract the lowest price from the highest price during the twelve months, and divide the difference by the annual low.)

$$\frac{high - low}{low}$$

ANNUAL HIGH	ANNUAL LOW	PERCENT
$65	$43	51%
37	34	9
45	41	10
35	25	4
84	62	35
71	68	4
118	101	17
154	112	38

FIGURE G.13. Volatility

volume the level of trading activity in a stock, an option, or in the market as a whole

wasting asset any asset that will decline in value over time (An option is a wasting asset because it will be worth its intrinsic value on expiration day, and worthless after expiration day.

writer the individual who sells—writes—a call

Index